Praise for *Without Oars*

"Reading Wes's remarkable pilgrimage, I found myself—somewhat like John, imprisoned on the isle of Patmos in the Bible—caught up 'in the Spirit,' there in the story, in the insights, in the wisdom, in the pilgrimage. I found myself 'lost in wonder, love and praise,' as the old hymn says. I sensed what the Bible calls 'the joyful liberty of the children of God.' Wow!"
— Rev. Michael Curry, Presiding Bishop and Primate, The Episcopal Church

"This book is really special. It's an adventure. You get all of Wes's great ideas, stories, and theology, but this time you feel like you are walking alongside him on the Camino. And he'll be inviting you to let go of some of the extra baggage so you're a little freer to enjoy the journey. This book will help you declutter your soul."
— Shane Claiborne, author, activist, and co-founder of Red Letter Christians

"Wesley Granberg-Michaelson describes the promise and joy of 'casting off into a life of pilgrimage' in ways that make us want to start walking. A wonderful book."
— Fr. Richard Rohr, director, Center for Action and Contemplation

"Compelling and beautifully written, Granberg-Michaelson's writing invites us into a deeper reality. Take the journey of reading *Without Oars* and experience the spiritual transformation and blossoming of the soul that await."
— Rev. Dr. Mae Elise Cannon, author of *Beyond Hashtag Activism: Comprehensive Justice in a Complicated Age*

"Up until now, when you think of spirituality and prayer, you may think of churches, sermons, organs, and words, words, words. If you dare to read this beautiful, courageous, and truly unforgettable book, you will think of feet, dirt, water, food, and dancing. As I read, I saw my past in a new light, and my present and future as well. This book stands out and gives extraordinary gifts."
— Brian D. McLaren, author of *The Galápagos Islands: A Spiritual Journey*

"Wes's pilgrim journey invites us into places of disruption, uncertainty, even surrender. He's a wise guide for this necessary journey. I commend this book to anyone who is open to discovering the treasure found in the detours and disruptions of an authentic faith journey."
—Chuck DeGroat, Professor of Pastoral Care and Christian Spirituality, Western Theological Seminary

"*Without Oars* is a lovely reminder that walking with Christ is a pilgrimage where we are accompanied and nourished in ways that touch the body and soul. This book is soothing and centering without ignoring the hard truths of our lives."
—Rev. Dr. Alexia Salvatierra, Professor of Development Studies, Fuller Theological Seminary

"In *Without Oars*, Wes Granberg-Michaelson shares the deep wisdom he has gained as a lifelong and contemplative pilgrim whose spiritual practice leads him to strong and effective social action for justice. This book is a genuine must-read for anyone who wants to apply faith to public life. I can't recommend it highly enough."
—Jim Wallis, Founder and President of Sojourners

"This enchanting book takes readers on a journey into the ancient and sacred terrain of Christian pilgrimage. Here we learn that pilgrimage is both a 'be-wilding,' external journey and an interior, mystical one."
—Cheryl Bridges Johns, Professor of Spiritual Renewal and Christian Formation, Pentecostal Theological Seminary

"*Without Oars* takes readers on an inspiring journey of rethinking Christian discipleship as an embodied reality rather than just a "belief in beliefs." There is no better guide for this excursion than Wesley Granberg-Michaelson, with his deep wisdom, pastoral sensitivity, and gift for storytelling."
—Dr. Kristin Colberg, College of St. Benedict/St. John's University

Without Oars

Without Oars

Casting Off
into a Life
of Pilgrimage

Wesley Granberg-Michaelson

 Broadleaf Books

Minneapolis

WITHOUT OARS
Casting Off into a Life of Pilgrimage

Published in association with Creative Trust Literary Group LLC, 320 Seven Springs Way, Suite 250, Brentwood, TN 37027, www.creativetrust.com.

Cover design and illustration by James Kegley
Back cover photograph © Kaarin Granberg-Michaelson. Used by permission.

Print ISBN: 978-1-5064-6434-3
eBook ISBN: 978-1-5064-6435-0

CONTENTS

FOREWORD

Writing a foreword for a book is a strange literary convention. One author adding words to another author's words is an awkward task at best. It is rather like designing a wedding invitation. The card that arrives in the mail, no matter how graceful or beautiful, how thoughtfully it expresses hopes and dreams, only beckons to the real event—the marriage celebration itself.

Without Oars is a celebration of spiritual maturity. I hope that does not seem stuffy or conservative. Sometimes talking about "maturity" can carry a whiff of finger-wagging superiority, especially toward those who are in a different place on life's journey. Yet the Christian tradition holds up spiritual maturity as the goal of life. It is a call to know the fullness of God. But what is it, really? And how does one get there?

There is a beautiful paradox in Christianity about the fullness of God—the paradox comes from the life of Jesus, the one who taught that we find our lives by losing them, and then drove the truth of the matter home through his own passion and death. Maturity comes by way of letting go, through loss. Fullness, depth, wisdom—whatever one calls it—is not a grim thing, however gloomy this paradox may seem. The letting go is a precursor to life. Christianity offers many paths to understand this—reading Scripture, contemplative prayer, serving one's neighbor, or the sacramental life of the church. But one of the most richly experiential ways into Christianity's central paradox has been the practice of pilgrimage. Pilgrims leave the comforts of home in order to find their true home. In *Without Oars,* Wes Granberg-Michaelson revisits this ancient practice by sharing his journey of walking the Camino de Santiago, a thousand-year-old pilgrim path in Spain.

What emerges in these pages is a sort of map, a way of letting go to find something new. I say "sort of map" because these chapters are not like a GPS, or an old-fashioned TripTik prepared by the auto club, and this is certainly not a "how-to" or "ten steps to" book. For the fundamental truth of the pilgrim is always the same: there might be a map—a route to a destination—but maps and guidebooks tell you little until your feet are on the ground. Ultimately, it is impossible to chart what the ancient Celtic saints called "wandering for the love of God." You have to walk to understand. Get up and go.

So what kind of map is opened in these pages? *Without Oars* does not tell you what particular road to take or where to turn. Instead, it shares what you can expect as you walk, like markers you see on some roadsides. How pilgrimages start with restlessness, how we are not really who we think we are, that patience is a gift, what we think makes us secure actually imprisons, faith is far more than we think, the Spirit is reckless, grace is always surprising, turning our backs on injustice is necessary on this road, and the end of all is love.

If this book were only a map, it would be like a wedding invitation. But it is more. Wes Granberg-Michaelson takes readers—insofar as is possible—into the event of walking. In Spain. At Lourdes. In Nigeria. Throughout New Mexico. At worship, in prayer, through stories of the Bible. With great economy of word, he lets you in as he lets go, and, in the process, you can let go, too. When you know you have a companion like this, you can breathe easier. For you are not alone on this way. You have a friend. Not a guide. A fellow walker.

And that makes it all the more believable, the path more joyful, to be together on the Way with others. To know that the Way is well trod and completely, beautifully unique; it is ancient and ever new. That we are beloved of God, the God who is the center of all things, and that the paradox leads toward the totality of love.

Diana Butler Bass
Alexandria, Virginia
Easter 2020

When you, the reader, dive into this book, it is impossible to know what our world will be like, what your life situation will be like. With political changes, global pandemics, we are entering new, unfamiliar territory, with outcomes often outside our desired control.

Perhaps you have picked up this book because you want to understand something about the passages of faith. Perhaps you will read this book alongside communities in turmoil. In whatever time and situation you find yourself, several things will likely be true: the spiritual life as a lifeline, patience as a necessity, and the need to discern what you will take into the future and what is best to leave behind. This attitude of discernment and dependence upon unpredictable grace, on God's Spirit, helps outline the path ahead.

Understanding faith as a pilgrimage, with all that this requires and promises, seems more than ever our "essential work," and not just an optional approach. We all will be walking our way into faith. I trust that the lessons to be learned, shared in these pages, will be more fruitful than ever for us all.

.

Prologue

In a Boat without Oars

On a gray, cold, rainy Thursday morning I sat at my wooden desk outside the senator's office, staring at the index card with Father Stephen's name and number on it. It had been sitting on my desk for weeks, like an exit ramp sign along the crowded highway of my life in DC.

Until now, I'd kept it in my peripheral vision. A friend, knowing I had been trying to nurture a spiritual journey of fits and starts, had suggested I consider going on retreat to the Trappist Holy Cross Monastery in nearby Berryville, Virginia.

I'd never been to a monastery before, much less a Trappist one. But I knew I needed to get away—maybe to someplace warm. My travel agent was ready to book a trip to the Virgin Islands. And although I didn't know why, I called the number on the card instead.

"This is Father Stephen."

"Hi, uh, I was wondering if you have a room available in the next few days for a retreat?" I asked, awkwardly.

"Come right away," he responded.

And so, without really knowing where I was going, physically or spiritually, I got in my car and drove away from the political turmoil in a new direction that changed the course of my life.

That was December of 1972, and I was physically and emotionally spent, having left it all on the field—in this case, the political playing field of that election year. At twenty-five years old, I was chief legislative assistant to Republican US Senator Mark O. Hatfield, who had just been reelected to his second term a month earlier. Two years before, as a leading opponent of the Vietnam War with Senator George McGovern, and as a courageous critic of President Richard Nixon, his future political career as a senator from Oregon had been in serious doubt. It was Hatfield's lonely and principled opposition to the war, and his deep Christian faith, that had compelled my endless hours of service. Now, his successful reelection meant that chapter could continue.

But I wasn't sure of my future. Having grown close to McGovern's staff in our antiwar efforts, I privately did all I could to support his presidential bid in 1972, including helping orchestrate McGovern's appearance and drafting his speech at Wheaton College, the "evangelical Harvard," during the campaign. But the outcome was a disaster, with McGovern losing forty-nine states to a triumphant Richard Nixon. The US political scene brought me to despair with the chants of "Four More Years" from Nixon's supporters ringing in my ears, while the crimes of Watergate were still mostly hidden.

What I didn't know at the time, but have learned since, is that decision to step away from all those pressures and drive my weary soul out to a Virginia monastery was an act of pilgrimage: a journey from the known to the unknown, from what no longer satisfied to a search for something life-giving.

We tend to think of pilgrimages as journeys to a specific destination—Santiago de Compostela, Rome, Lourdes, Jerusalem, Trondheim, and more. But as much as they might be about place, they are also equally about what the pilgrim leaves behind, propelled by an inward journey.

"It is good once in a while to feel oneself in the hands of God," Søren Kierkegaard once wrote, "and not always eternally slinking around the familiar nooks and corners of a town where one always knows the way out." That's the yearning that pushes pilgrims out the door, physically or spiritually, stepping away from home in order to search for the soul's true home.

Perhaps because it intentionally lacks any grand strategy or compelling plan, there is a spiritual compulsion, so inexplicable to modern, rationalistic understanding, to embark on pilgrimage. A modern Irish global pilgrim, U2's Bono, catches something of this in the song title "Running to Stand Still." And movement is always essential. You set out. You begin to walk, or sail, or drive, taking what you can for an unknown timeline, and leaving all the rest behind. You don't wait for an itinerary.

That's how pilgrimages usually start. You are feeling dissatisfied, anxious, depleted, desperate, or just deeply discontented. In such a moment, you know that your present circumstances of life are simply not working. There's a longing for something more, something different, something deeper. But you are not sure of what this is. Asked to describe what you are seeking by a friend or therapist, your answers become vague and tentative. The yearning comes more at the intuitive level. You have discovered an inner thirst that can't be quenched by the outward circumstances of your life. Usually it requires a decision to take a step out of the accustomed and superficially comfortable normalcy of your present reality. And leave it behind.

Billy Graham had a weekly radio show titled *The Hour of Decision*. Normally it was a tape recording of the service and message he'd given at a recent evangelistic rally. And at the conclusion of every message, Graham would issue an invitation for anyone to make a commitment to Jesus Christ, and to do so by getting up out of their seat and making their way to the front, where Graham had been preaching. Coming forward, Graham would say, was an outward demonstration of this inner desire. He insisted that those so moved would take these physical steps to begin a new spiritual journey. This was, for them, the hour of decision.

Billy Graham was tapping into something perhaps even deeper than he knew. Any time a person feels prompted to leave the present in order to embrace a new pathway in life, a decision is required. It's not a decision just made in the head, or even the heart; it's something embodied. It requires a physical step forward, leaving behind our desk, or friends, or comforts as we start to walk, vulnerably, into an unknown future.

As a teenager, I used to watch television broadcasts of Graham's rallies, fascinated to see those getting up out of their seats start walking. Were they scared, or troubled, or distraught, or joyful? What was moving through their hearts? How many felt they were walking into an unknown future, but simply had to take those steps in this sudden hour of decision?

Many have studied what happened to those seekers. But that, and the theology encapsulating Graham's rallies, is another story. What intrigues me is the point where a person gets up and starts to move, leaving friends, relatives, and normal expectations behind. The body begins the journey of change. Religious faith is an embodied journey, not a protected cocoon of beliefs. It's a pilgrimage.

Here's a true story, from the year 891, of those who cast off in an embodied journey to live "in a state of pilgrimage, for the love of God." Three Irish pilgrims, Dubslane, Macbeth, and Maelinmun, made the dramatic decision to set out into the ocean from their homeland in a boat purposely "without oars." Their destination was in God's hands, or, more precisely, in God's breath. In Hebrew, *wind*, *breath*, and *Spirit* are all the same word. Their boat was made of two and a half hides, and they took provisions for seven days. On the seventh night they landed in Cornwall, in what today is the southwestern tip of England, convinced that they were precisely where they were meant to be.

There's a Latin term that captures both their purpose and experience and that of hundreds like them: "*peregrinatio pro amore Dei*," or "wandering for the love of God." Many pilgrims from Ireland had gone before, departing without external destinations, but guided by interior journeys. Trying to explain their motivation, one author says they were "seeking the place of one's resurrection." Such pilgrims felt compelled to do so, often against all odds.

The account of St. Columbanus is among these *peregrinatio* stories. In 591 with twelve companions he left Ireland. He and his companions severed themselves from family and country on an uncharted spiritual trek through the European continent. The result of their wandering for the love of God was a string of monasteries established through today's France, Germany, Switzerland, and Italy.

Some of these pilgrim journeys seem too good to be true. St. Brendan of Clonfert set sail to the west of Ireland, rather than the east, with seventeen monks on a wandering seafaring journey not for seven days, but seven years. This became the stuff of legends. A fantastical account, the *Navigatio*, circulated in numerous languages throughout

Europe centuries later, something like perhaps *The Lord of the Rings*. Separating fiction from truth seemed hardly the point. This pilgrim tale captured popular imagination, and St. Brendan became known as the "Navigator" and the "Voyager." The spirit of this seven-year pilgrim saga can be heard in the instructions to his men: "The Lord is our captain and helmsman is He not? Then let Him direct us where He wills." And there is enough truth in the stories of Brendan to gain his image in a stained-glass window at the United States Naval Academy.

Historians like Thomas Cahill in *How the Irish Saved Civilization* shed new light on how different waves of these Irish pilgrims on their missionary journeys kept alive the sparks of Western civilization and Christian faith during an era of cultural and spiritual deterioration in Europe. And this, coming with no grand strategy, no coordination of these disparate pilgrimage adventures, no compelling mission plan.

For these Celts, setting out "without oars" radically focused attention on an interior destination. The sagas of these early Irish pilgrims were marked by physical and spiritual abandonment as they cast off from those shores and the security of home and family. From the first, and then as these pilgrim wanderers were exposed to physical danger, there was nothing and no one left to trust but God.

That first inexplicable visit to Holy Cross Monastery in 1972 led to many more, with Father Stephen becoming a trusted friend and spiritual director. As I waded into the contemplative tradition it resonated with my soul. Somehow, it had much more integrity and reflective transparency than the evangelical piety of my upbringing. Or maybe I was just attracted to the captivating and inspiring novelty of Thomas Merton's story and words.

In any event, by early 1974 I took a month off from my continuing work with Mark Hatfield, responding to an invitation to live in a monastic room with the Trappist monks at Berryville, sharing their rhythms of prayer, silence, meals, and work, beginning at 3:30 each morning. I once broke the silence to ask Father Stephen, at 3:15 over instant coffee in the refectory, how he ever got used to rising so early. "I haven't," came his chanted reply.

Because of that ongoing journey, in times that followed I couldn't quench a growing inner restlessness toward the outward circumstances of my life. Finally, my wife, Kaarin, and I decided to set off on our own pilgrimage, leaving behind the security of life in Washington, DC.

The sign on the back of our small trailer read "Missoula or Bust." By the time our lumbering Ford reached Wyoming, our pilgrimage almost did bust. Driving the one hundred miles from Gillette to Sheridan in the evening we hit a blizzard. In 1979 there was little on I-90 between those two cities; Kaarin and I genuinely feared not making it and getting stranded. I've been afraid to drive in snowstorms ever since.

We were not only leaving DC; we were also leaving plans and people deeply important to us: the newly formed Sojourners community and magazine, a health clinic begun by Kaarin, and my dreams of an ongoing political career.

Unlike those Celtic pilgrims in their oarless boat, we did have a destination—Missoula, Montana. But we had no outcome, job, or plan apart from getting a dog and living with a church community there. In our pockets we had three months of income with the rest unaccounted for. I knew I wanted to try to *be* rather than *do*, at least for a while. Both Kaarin and I were searching for a place of resurrection without at least some of the oars we had relied upon. Our journey had abruptly begun on another course, with the unexpected destinations that followed.

Thirty-nine years later, on one predawn morning, I set off yet again. Quietly slipping out of my bed in the hostel, I put on my gear and headed out in the dark, a small L.L. Bean spotlight attached to my cap. I felt like a miner preparing to descend into a mineshaft.

I walked in darkness, awaiting the dawn and (I hoped) coffee. But I had no idea what the day would bring. The terrain was unknown, and the pathway at times uncertain despite the ubiquitous yellow arrows painted on pavement, walls, and trees. The places and pilgrims encountered were mysteriously unpredictable.

As the day brought the heat of August, I heard the encouraging words "Buen camino" called out from locals in cafés, hostels, and churches as I walked 135 miles as a pilgrim on the way to Santiago de Compostela in northern Spain. My three colleagues and I had a destination, the same one shared by millions of pilgrims over these pathways for the past one thousand years—the Cathedral of Santiago de Compostela, which by legend holds the bones of the apostle James.

Most "oars" were left behind—first and foremost, simply conveyance. I was walking as never before in my life, depending on nothing more than my legs and the determination of my soul. Another oar we left behind was time. Normally measured in minutes and punctuated by appointments, life was somehow suspended. Minutes and hours past flowed into my journey, rather than my days being marked by the clock's progression.

The normal comforts of everyday travel were left in another life. My body was exhausted as I continually sucked water from my CamelBak; my feet were tired and sore. What awaited wasn't a Marriott Courtyard; rather it was an albergue, a hostel for pilgrims, with bunks sharing sixteen to sixty in a room. I walked to the sounds of water, wind, sometimes cars and trucks, and the voices of other pilgrims periodically encountered. Absent was the noise normally reverberating in my head—the onslaught of news, the intellectual entertainment of NPR, and the perpetual assault of email and texts. Silence became my regular companion.

As I took daily footsteps into the unexpected, I began to anticipate the surprising intrusion of moments of grace and tried to trust in them. Rarely did I think of *getting* to Santiago de Compostela; rather, I focused on where my steps would lead before the next break for water, coffee, or food.

Leaving behind one's oars and nurturing amnesia about a target destination opens life, I was learning, to the immediate wonder of the present. It shed light into the mineshafts of my heart, with its joys and pains.

At this point in my pilgrimage, I'm trying to leave everything behind but Jesus. In the United States that commitment has become publicly problematic. Why? It's because of the obnoxious behavior of many Christians and their churches, along with countless white evangelicals displaying more loyalty to versions of exclusive nationalism than to the words and way of Jesus. This has made a mockery of their "brand" within society, where all who claim this pilgrim way are also burdened with this nasty, unwanted baggage. Allegedly defined by mutual love, the self-righteous judgment and exclusion of LGBTQ persons from fellowship has driven a younger generation away from the church in droves. It's no wonder that in the US those who claim no religious faith now surpass the number of those describing themselves as "evangelical."

What does it mean, then, and what is required to embark on a new and uncertain pilgrimage through a landscape of faith that others have defined? And what does it mean to embark on that pilgrimage through the public square?

In an effort to "reclaim Jesus," I've journeyed with a group of "elders." Led by Michael Curry, presiding bishop of the Episcopal Church, and Jim Wallis, we drafted a confession of faith during the age of Trump that tried to make sense of Jesus, with a video that went viral. So many have been listening and yearning for a different way to follow Jesus in a schismatic time.

It's hard to follow Jesus. I used to think following depended on believing right doctrine and truths. But at this point in my journey, doctrine is overrated. It resides in the head, not in the body, not in the soul. Creeds are a curious legacy of a search for a safe harbor of rational religious certitudes. Those certainties have ended up slaughtering hundreds of thousands—violence of Christians and against Christians. Yes, some foundational truths about Christian faith are important. But a lot fewer than I thought.

What I do know now is that we need to learn how to walk our way into faith on a pilgrimage that shapes and defines our whole lives and not just our thought. Pilgrimage serves as a powerful metaphor for understanding the journey of faith. This is something John Bunyan knew when he wrote *The Pilgrim's Progress* in 1678, at one time second only to the Bible in popularity. It continues to be the best-known allegory of Christian faith ever in print. But beyond the words and allegories, it's the actual practice of pilgrimage I'm captivated by. Over the centuries, millions of people have given expression to their faith, and their search for God, not through what they believed, but by where they walked.

On the Camino de Santiago, makeshift shrines along the way are littered with things pilgrims have left behind— an extra pair of shoes, a sweater, a razorblade, an inflatable pillow, a book, a pair of pants, a makeup kit. Nearly every pilgrim on the Camino, despite careful packing, discovers that they are carrying too much. Once walking for a while, they feel weighed down by too much stuff crammed into their packs. Unburdening themselves of what is no longer deemed essential, they move forward with a lighter pack, a freer spirit. This process of shedding is liberating.

One of the crucial first steps in the spiritual discernment process is called "shedding." In *Discerning God's Will Together*, Danny Morris and Charles M. Olsen offer steps for discernment as an alternative way of decision-making. In contrast to rational debate, majority voting, and parliamentary procedures, I've used these at times of crucial decision-making. Shedding is a spiritual commitment to leave behind all our preconceived ideas, arguments, agendas, and biases, holding them in suspense, while asking only one question: "Am I indifferent to everything but God's will?"

Such shedding, so contrary to the typical practice of adding up one's most forceful arguments, is essential to discerning the outcome of a difficult matter through probing, embedded spiritual attention. What opens up is beyond the rational: novel and unexpected directions.

Shedding—losing our oars—can lead to a different kind of certainty. Instead of piling on more words or propositions or goods or comforts, we begin to let them go, and leave them behind, encountering deeper truth. Relinquishing what has weighed us down, we walk mysteriously toward that home for our heart, a home near God.

So, the way of the pilgrim begins with what they leave behind. That's not the common way we think about pilgrimages, but it is foundational. And this is no onetime action. In an ongoing way, pilgrimage requires relinquishment at physical, emotional, theological, cultural, and spiritual levels. As we step forward, we are asked to take another nonessential item out of the pack we have been carrying on our backs, in our heads, or within our hearts.

Like items left along the path, encountering what we leave behind as we walk into future faith is like moving through concentric circles. Passing through one circle we are presented with another, beckoning us ahead but asking us to unload something else, and revealing more mystery and depth with each step forward. A pilgrimage is a spiritual and physical practice to ground our life in the messy, arduous, joyful, endless, grace-filled path of following the Way. No oars. A lightened pack.

I ask myself, What makes this pilgrimage difficult? And I hear the answer: I carry so much accumulated stuff. I don't mean just material things; my wife and I discover that as the years go by, we just naturally seem to do with a little less. But all my life I've carried weighty theological assertions—creeds and historic confessions I declared were faithful interpretations of the Bible. These I took into my pack when I was ordained.

I'm weighed down, too, with psychological baggage, carrying insecurities about these final chapters in my journey. Daily I carry political baggage: the weight of tribal politics, and the politics of my tribe. I carry the burden and reality of my ethno-European histories of oppression, of my whiteness, still trying to understand the subtle paths of privilege that have always marked my journey. My pilgrim path beckons me to unpack these weighty realities, leave behind what I can, and carry lightly what I need as I seek simply to follow Jesus.

Each of our journeys carries baggage that is overweight. And it can't be checked and placed out of sight and mind. These bags are carry-on, and they won't all fit. So we ask ourselves, What should be left behind? And in that process of asking and unpacking, we discover not deprivation, but liberation and joy.

What does being in a boat without oars truly require? In these pages we'll explore the concentric circles marking *peregrinatio pro amore Dei*: which weights are left behind, and the experiences of joy and liberation that are discovered, as the pilgrim steps forward and follows. I've identified ten movements forward. And the embodied experiences of actual pilgrimages, both present and in history, will ground this literary journey and hopefully give you wind, courage, and the relinquishment to cast off into your own pilgrimage.

My journey has taken me on pilgrim paths not only to Santiago de Compostela, but to Lourdes, France; Chimayó, New Mexico; Ogere Remo, Nigeria; and elsewhere. Few of us have the time, resources, or invitations to make even one of these kinds of journeys in a lifetime. I'm aware of the privilege and responsibility that comes with that gift as well as the understanding that pilgrimages don't depend on famous destinations or even travel further than our own locales. Pilgrimages start for each of us right where we are, beckoning us to go forward, without oars.

There's a story in the gospels about Jesus calling his first disciples. He goes to the seashore, finds fishermen Simon Peter and Andrew, and calls them to follow. For reasons we can only imagine, they choose to do so. And with that decision to follow, they immediately "leave their nets behind." James and John are then called, and they respond by leaving their boats and their father behind (Matt. 4:18–22). Even here the pattern is clear: a step forward, into an unknown pilgrimage, requires us to shed normal securities.

Many of us stay embedded in nets and networks that define us and can entrap us. Yet each of us can identify times when a call on our smartphone, or a text, or a conversation, or a movie, or a crisis, suddenly offered a step forward and a way out.

This book is about meeting that unexpected opportunity and asking whether we can leave our nets behind, get up, and start walking.

Chapter 1

The Restless Soul

Pilgrimages usually mean walking. It's the most abrupt change from one's normal routine. All of life is slowed down, and one is liberated from a daily bondage to speed. Walking is usually the most inefficient way to get from one destination to another. But it frees one, even in subconscious ways, from the obligation to get everything done fast. It also opens an entirely different view of the physical world. What if we walked? On the Camino de Santiago, after our day's journey, we arrived at our albergue in Villafranca del Bierzo, were assigned to our bunk beds, welcomed mostly cold showers, hung up underwear we had washed, and headed out in search of dinner.

A sign on the wall of the albergue in Villafranca reminded us of our purpose: "El Camino es tiempo de meditación interior; no itinerario turístico." The Camino is a time for interior meditation, not a tourist route.

The next day would be arduous. We faced a steep hill, one of the highest of our ten-day journey, but it led into

Galicia, the northern province of Spain that was shaped by Celtic influences. Two-thirds of the way up the mountain, the tiny village of La Faba has an albergue run by a German group in support of the Camino, with thirty-five beds. We would try to make it there.

The following morning, once more reminded "El Camino es tiempo de meditación interior; no itinerario turístico," we started the path to La Faba, covering twenty-five kilometers. In Vega de Valcarce, before the ascent up the mountain, I stopped in the church of St. John the Baptist to look, reflect, and pray. The trek that followed up the rocky path of the hillside, bordered by chestnut trees, was hard. I didn't know if my knees would hold up. Each step, at points, was a journey. I finally arrived late that afternoon at the albergue and its adjoining church, where I was met by my younger, swifter companions, whom I had urged to go ahead.

One can drive from Villafranca del Bierzo to La Faba. The drive takes twenty-one minutes. That's the normal way, and a completely different journey. On the Camino, distance and time become entirely new experiences, created by walking. You experience both the gifts and the pain of the terrain—the bright sky and a slippery, steep rocky path. To walk away from your normal routine is to intentionally open your life to the space and time for an interior journey.

Kosuke Koyama was a Japanese theologian and missionary to Thailand who developed theology from within his Asian context. Forty years ago he wrote *Three Mile an Hour God*, which the walking pilgrim understands well. In it he writes:

God walks "slowly" because he is love. If he is not love he would have gone much faster. Love has its speed. It is an inner speed. It is a spiritual speed. It is a different kind of speed from the technological speed to which we are accustomed. It is "slow" yet it is lord over all other speeds since it is the speed of love. It goes on in the depth of our life, whether we notice or not, whether we are currently hit by storm or not, at three miles an hour. It is the speed we walk and therefore it is the speed the love of God walks.

As a Protestant, for decades I've been stealing Jesus at Catholic Masses. I did so again at the Real Iglesia Parroquial de Santiago y San Juan Bautista in Madrid, Spain, before starting my Camino. The Mass was at noon, followed by a blessing for pilgrims.

Five of us, from different countries, came to the front altar, where the priest led us in a liturgy, praying for our pilgrimage and sending us forth. We were being commissioned and blessed for our journey. I didn't know the others. But each of us was restless enough or compelled enough to walk away from the regularity of our lives. The paths beckoning our steps were unknown to us but traversed by countless pilgrims on the Camino over a millennium. In medieval times, when a person decided to go on a pilgrimage to Rome, Jerusalem, or Santiago de Compostela, they were leaving everything behind, and not certain of their return.

Often, they would settle debts, draw up a will, and see that their affairs were in order. Walking out of their city gate, a life of predictable routines and dependable relationships was dramatically broken. Dress changed, of course, with a cloak, satchel, staff, and hat designed for their journey and marking them apart. Those who traveled were often blessed by a priest at a service, reminiscent of the one I attended, prior to departure.

The day before, I had arrived in Madrid, bleary-eyed from eighteen hours of flights and layovers. Checking in at a small hotel, I shared my trip's purpose. The desk clerk, Uxoa, broke into a broad smile. "I've done the Camino," she exclaimed. "It was the best experience of my life!" The Camino intervenes and disrupts, with unexpected affirmations.

Once I checked in, I found a church for Mass in a square not far from the Royal Palace, but off the normal tourist track. Its stately but plain exterior was in marked contrast to the ornate carvings, paintings, and altar within, including a striking statue of a medieval pilgrim.

An office off the sanctuary gives pilgrims an official "Credencial." This small booklet the size of a passport with numerous pages folding out, each with eight squares, becomes the documentary proof of a pilgrim's journey. Along the way, the pilgrim stops at churches, inns, hostels, hotels, bars, and restaurants on the Camino, receiving official stamps registering the journey, stop by stop.

Pilgrimages always begin with this: a decision to break the normal routine. Of course, we break our routines in many ways. Vacations do so, although we often carry our smart-phones and our normal work with us. We can "take a break" in any number of ways, for leisure or retreat or rejuvenation.

But a pilgrimage breaks with normal predictability in a very specific way: not to fill life with other activity, but to empty life of former activities. It pulls away the veneer of time-absorbing routines. What lies beneath is often unknown. It requires walking out the gates that circum-scribe the normal predictability of our lives.

Just walking helps. Our normal routines are not only pre-dictable, but also fast paced. Western culture and its highly competitive economic and social systems seem to have done something extraordinary—they have increased the speed of time. At least that's how it feels. And as any therapist would say, feelings are real. Those of us in modern culture feel that time moves fast. We even say it: "Time flies." To sell a prod-uct, or to win an athletic contest, one must gain an edge. This means searching for a way for something to get done faster and more efficiently.

Time gets commodified. It's measured for its value, bro-ken into parcels, and farmed out. It must be used in ways that maximize its utility, increasing the profits that can be reaped. So, we live our lives fast. Many of our routines are designed to accommodate the pace of living in the fast lane. When we eat, when we work out, and when we sleep become ways of adjusting to the continual and rapid press of expec-tations from our work, or our children, or our spouses, or all of these. We can't waste time, and we move fast just to get by. We're driven and sometimes crippled by the fear of falling behind.

Conveyance, of course, is an essential part of a life that seems governed by speed. The crunch of time means you must move as fast as you can, at an acceptable cost, from one place to another. Automobiles remain the primary means to do so, and for most Americans they are an indispensable part of life's fast-paced routines. The US is home to about 270 million passenger vehicles; that's about 833 vehicles for every one thousand people. New Zealand has about the same percentage. Of all the world's nations, only Monaco and San Marino are higher. As Americans we are addicted to our cars. And locomotion by means of one's own body and the pace of that makes walking a radical break from normalcy.

Disruptions from normalcy can erupt from inner stirrings that can't be repressed. I awoke one morning at 5:30 at our home in Santa Fe with my soul restless and my heart distressed by a two-hour late-night phone conversation with a dear friend. My day was set with a swimming exercise class, two scheduled telephone calls, and pressing responses required from a pastoral search process I was heading in our congregation. But a deeper and disquieting movement in my spirit beckoned me. In the early morning, after I wake, I regularly sit and engage in combat between meditation and slumber. By

6:10 a.m. an idea was taking hold. If I quickly got dressed and into my car, I could get to the Benedictine monastery in Pecos, New Mexico, by the start of the Eucharist at 7:30 a.m. I left, and left the rest of my planned day behind.

Our Lady of Guadalupe Abbey has become a periodic landing place for my soul since arriving to live in Santa Fe. The Pecos River and the trout it holds flow down the valley bearing its name and through the grounds of the monastery, whose rustic, simple adobe style blends into the landscape. After I arrived in the chapel, with its striking tile mosaic of Our Lady of Guadalupe, the Abbot, Father Aiden, welcomed me from the sacristy where he was robing and invited me to the community's simple breakfast following the eucharistic meal we were about to receive.

I had come because I needed to be centered, to know how to respond to the turmoil confronting my friend, to understand what was needed, now, to be a true friend. A decisive interruption broke the expected routine of that day. And I was at the Pecos Monastery, so I fell into the routine I typically used to structure my time there when going for retreat. Clarity about my response began to emerge. I went to the simple lounge, with its classic vinyl leather Western couch and chair bearing the design of a cactus, and a Bunn coffeemaker that continually heats brewed coffee in its glass pitcher until it is aged to that distinctive charred, acrid flavor.

I searched for the network "Monastery" and entered the password "Monastery Guest." It's an exception to the Benedictine Rule of Life, tempting retreatants with the option of remaining connected to their other worlds. I settled in and wrote an email capturing what I needed to say. And then I walked.

I walked along the Pecos River, gauging the clarity of its water and looking for living streams within. Then I walked up to Monastery Lake, watching others who had come and sat by the shore, fishing.

Walking slowed down my mind, and my day. More became clear about how courageous truth-telling can solidify rather than jeopardize a treasured friendship. These periodic breaks—mere steps—in search of breakthroughs are like mini pilgrimages. The first step, in every case, is a decision to interrupt the routine of one's day, or week, or year, or life. Again and again, our insistent restlessness interrupts ingrained routines in order to create the open space necessary for an interior journey.

There's a difference, of course, in steps of redirection from, say, mindfulness or attention to the presence of grace in the commonplace. In my twenties, when I was a member of Church of the Saviour, I was introduced to the small book by Brother Lawrence, *The Practice of the Presence of God*. Born in France around 1610, Brother Lawrence was injured and crippled in the Thirty Years' War, when he was still known as Nicholas Herman. Drawn to the spiritual life, he entered a new monastery established in Paris and became the cook for its one hundred members. Amidst the ordinary routines of the kitchen, Brother Lawrence developed a continual practice of attentiveness to God's presence.

After his death, his letters were collected and published in a small pamphlet that became a spiritual classic. Serving coffee to guests on Thursday evenings at the Church of the Saviour's Potter's House during those years, I tried to "practice the presence," as I did in the DC offices of my professional work.

Yes (emphatically), God's grace can intervene when we pour coffee, work, and take out the garbage. But we still are pouring coffee, working, and taking out the garbage. The odors, interruption, attention, and annoyances can keep us preoccupied with the mundane things of life. It is that which interrupts everything in our routines that is normally the first step to opening the path for a pilgrimage, despite the sound of the garbage truck coming down the alley.

Organizations can also embark on pilgrimages. After all, organizations, congregations, and groups are living organisms. When they regard themselves as static and largely unchanging entities, they are likely to atrophy and die. The reality is that organizations can evolve, grow, and move. Such healthy growth begins with interruptions that open space where pilgrimage becomes as important as long-range planning.

Recent thinking about organizational leadership, in fact, stresses how effective leaders are not those who perfect predictable systems of strategic planning. Rather, they they are those who create interruptions, or, in the parlance, *disruptions,* in the normal routines of business and activity for dynamic growth.

Among those who have studied patterns of leadership and organizational changes is Dr. Donde A. Plowman, now chancellor at the University of Tennessee, Knoxville. Over a decade ago, she and several colleagues published an article in *Leadership Quarterly,* titled "The Role of Leadership in Emergent, Self-Organization."

When gifted leaders learned how to break normal patterns and disrupt predictable expectations, Plowman and the others discovered, change and growth in organizations resulted. This created space for novelty to emerge, even in the face of uncertainties about eventual outcomes. As I read the article, I understood that—in very different terms—it spoke to the grounds for transformation remarkably like the process of beginning a pilgrimage.

Illustrating the concept, Plowman's team described their five-year research of a large downtown church—they named it "Mission Church" to protect anonymity—that was struggling to maintain vitality. Taking actions that were clearly disruptive, risky, and unpredictable, the congregation centered itself around the city's homeless population and embarked on a journey to seek a new future.

The eventual but direct result was a revitalized, growing congregation that had broken with its past, on a pilgrimage that discovered a fresh sense of its calling reverberating through its life.

The story and the theory that it supports match my own experience of organizational leadership as well as my growing understanding that the ancient practice of pilgrimage is transformative for the individual. Consider how the overwhelming desire of board members to balance the budget and keep to formal structures reports a stability for nonprofit organizations or congregations that is frequently deceptive. In many cases, the leader's desire to avoid conflict and provide a relentlessly positive spin on reports destabilizes prospects for transformational change that might erupt (if allowed) from below the surface.

The comfort of doing business as usual is a veneer that must be peeled away to open the space for essential exploration and growth. It takes a pilgrimage to renew an organization. And leaders with courage interrupt normal proceedings and disrupt comfortable, predictable expectations.

Considered a "caretaker pontiff," Pope John XXIII, three months after the smoke arose from the Vatican to declare him pope, changed course. On January 25, 1959, he stunned the Catholic and larger religious, ecumenical communities by announcing that a Second Ecumenical Council of the church would be convened. The pope said it was time "to open the windows [of the church] and let in some fresh air." Nothing of this kind had happened for one hundred years.

Meeting in sessions from 1962 to 1965, Vatican II brought fundamental changes to the life of the church, a church encompassing one-half of all the world's Christians, in every sphere: how the church worshipped, what liturgies and styles it welcomed, which languages it used for Mass, whom Catholics could pray with, how Catholics should relate to those of other religious faiths, what the challenges of the modern world meant for Catholic faith, and so much more. Over two thousand people participated in producing sixteen documents meant to establish fresh directions for the church.

None of this would have been possible if Pope John XXIII had not interrupted the normal routines of the church and disrupted its expectations by initiating this ecclesial pilgrimage. Six decades later, with the disruptive leadership of Pope Francis, the Catholic Church is confronting deeply serious challenges to its vitality and integrity. But this half of the Christian family would have rapidly atrophied without the reforms of Vatican II. Whether dealing with Vatican, the largest Christian organization in the world, or a small struggling nonprofit in Lincoln, Nebraska, that challenge is the same. If our attention is always captured by the dictates of normal routines, we'll miss the moments of promise unlocking a fresh future. It takes a courageous, disruptive first step to embark on a pilgrimage into uncharted territory that may discover new life.

When Muslims conquered Spain in the eighth century, Christians who adopted Arabic language and culture but maintained the practice of Christianity were called Mozarabs. In 812, years prior to the advent of the Camino de Santiago, this Mozarabic prayer conveyed the essence of what it means to be called forth on a pilgrimage:

You call us from our settled ways, O God,
*   out of old habits and rutted traditions.*
You call us into the land of promise,
*   to new life and new possibilities.*
Make us strong to travel the road ahead.
Deliver us from false security and comfort,
*   desire for ease and uninvolved days.*
Let your Word and Spirit dwell in us
*   that your will may be fulfilled in us*
*   for the well-being and shalom of all. Amen.*

Chapter 2

Real Presence

"We have more and more information, and less and less understanding," the late James Billington, august librarian of Congress, once told me. For twenty-eight years he navigated the explosion of information, expanding the Library of Congress's collections from 85 million items to more than 160 million, and he brought that institution into the digital age. Billington first shared this observation with me years before, when he was a professor at Princeton University, and also a mentor and friend when I studied at Princeton Seminary. The truth of those words has expanded exponentially since then.

We absorb this information, increasingly, by our smart, mobile phones. They connect us as never before to people, events, news, directions, facts, music, fashion, sports, stores, markets, flights, and politics. Most interests, activities, and needs are accessed through our phones, whose apps are portals delivering a constant avalanche of information. In our pockets, in our hands, or on our belts, they function like human appendages. Amputation is painful.

iPhones have Screen Time, a feature that measures the extent of my addiction to this device. I looked at the report for my last seven days. Two hours and forty-four minutes average screen time per day, an increase of 12 percent from the week before. The week's total came in at nineteen hours and fifteen minutes, heightened by watching parts of various Cubs games. Three hundred times that week I checked my phone. These are called "Pickups," averaging forty-three times a day. On Monday, I activated my screen sixty-three times to look at something. Taking those periods when I was awake, that meant I was picking up my phone four times an hour. It's at my bedside, charging. Waking at 3:15 a.m. to go to the bathroom, at times I'll check my phone, for I don't know what.

The first cell phone call was made by a Motorola engineer, Marty Cooper, in 1973. It was received with skepticism, like cartoon character Dick Tracy's radio wristwatch. Another decade would pass before it was developed and marketed. Today, smartphones captivate our attention, distract our thoughts, and intrude into any journey toward the solitude of the soul.

Ubiquitous information brought to our fingertips assaults reflective understanding. Whether Fox, CNN, or MSNBC, banners of "breaking news" flash across the screen with the next sensational story before we've even thought about the last one. The need to access information right as it unfolds is why journalists and many others cannot live without Twitter. News cycles now are pressure cookers, constantly compressing new information into dissected soundbites, creating combustible mixtures of reaction and counterreaction to keep eyes attached to screens.

The information revolution, spurred by the incredible ability of the internet to make any desired facts and forays directly accessible to personalized screens, was supposed to liberate us. In many ways it has. But it also imprisons us. We become locked into the insatiable desire for more factoids, more texts, more likes, more friends, more pictures, and more notifications, handcuffing us to our devices.

The modern pilgrim learns to walk away from screens, thirsting for real presence.

The constant threads, headlines, and enmeshed social networks in the online world are not simply distracting inordinate amounts of our attention. We often project a superficial, false self into the virtual world that we curate through our pictures, our likes, our posts, our tweets, and our profiles. Our screen time protects and nurtures this false self as we market ourselves to our "friends." Walking away from this superficial self, with its subtle but insatiable desire to be liked, often means taking distance from our screens.

Darker realities also ensue, requiring a posture of suspicion and a discipline of distance. We share our tastes, hobbies, trips, books, political views, sports loyalties, and so much more about our lives online to connect with others. But all this information and more beyond our awareness is sucked up by companies to use for their commercial gain. These treasure troves of personal data are the currency of the companies that drive the internet.

Companies learn what we like, where we go, and how we think in order to better exploit us for their profit. Ad revenue is driven by the frequency and duration that our eyes are on screens. Internet companies working on this model have an incentive to make our online presence as addictive as possible and have perfected the means to do so.

In a survey of 2,300 mobile phone users in the US and the UK, over one-third felt their phone usage was having a negative effect on their health and well-being. So, the ubiquity and power of our screens provoke some counter-measures—commitments to limit our time, or that of our teenagers. We ban phones from family dinners. We seek a "fast" from social media. We employ apps to restrain our use of other apps. But most of those attempts gradually falter. Even if they do reduce times of attachment to screens, they don't automatically nurture the space to replace the mere absorption of unbounded information with the reflection and understanding longed for by James Billington.

This "irresistible attraction to screens is leading people to feel as though they're ceding more and more of their autonomy when it comes to deciding how they direct their attention." So writes Cal Newport in *Digital Minimalism*. That threat should pierce our hearts. Who or what decides where our attention goes? As apps on our phones now deliver podcasts and uninterrupted music to us anywhere, we are "provided for the first time the ability to be *continuously* distracted from [our] own mind[s]." Recognizing the reality of this addiction, Newport advocates a thirty-day period of total abstinence in order to then build a more self-directed, restrained use of our devices.

How do we overcome omniscient distractions and find the self-directed agency to discover real presence, first of all, to our true selves? That's the burning question. But centuries before screens, contemplatives asked and then answered the same question, not with rational responses, but with embodied practices.

For ages, men and women living as monks, cloistered nuns, hermits, and wandering pilgrims have mastered the art of turning loneliness into solitude, creating a real presence to themselves, and to God. Their lessons and practices are not cloistered today; they offer liberating tools that can resurrect and protect the space for real presence for all who desire detachment from the omnipresence of screens. Simply consider this: you can't walk on unexpected pathways while looking at screens.

The "classic" experience of the Camino de Santiago today begins in France at St. Jean Pied de Port, at the base of the Pyrenees, as featured in the movie *The Way* with

Martin Sheen. It usually takes pilgrims thirty to thirty-five days to walk the 480 miles to Santiago de Compostela from St. Jean Pied de Port.

As I approached the portion of the Camino I was walking, I thought it would be a convenient sabbatical from my screen. I began to think about loopholes. Music, I thought. What about listening to music? The chants of Taizé, music of Marty Haugen—I had already started to build my playlist. As I was planning to go, I asked my wife's cousin, Mark Van Oss, who had walked the Camino from St. Jean and inspired my pilgrimage, about music. Mark demurred. Better, he advised, to just be fully present to all the sights and sounds encountered on the way.

How many steps does it take to clear the mind? It takes time, and often thousands of steps. Our smartphones mimic our minds in some ways. On my iPhone, when I go to a site and view what's on the screen and then go to another site, the first screen keeps functioning in the background. This happens continually, and eventually the memory gets crowded. What helps is to press twice on the control button at the bottom of the phone, and then all the previous screens still running will appear in a staggered sequence. Then, with your finger you flip each screen to the top, and it is cleared. You do this until no screen but the present one is functioning.

Our minds are constantly distracted by what we've seen, or done. Or remembered. All these things hum in our brains, absorbing pervasive information, messages, music.

From a perpetually distracted mind, it is difficult to find a centered mind, our true self. The invitation to walk brings us to a place where we can slowly clear away the constant preoccupations running in the background, and sometimes the foreground, of our minds. We are invited to, step by step, dropped oar by dropped oar, let them go, allow them to slip off our internal screens, empty ourselves of crowding distractions, and open up interior space. That's when our mind can catch its breath, or God's breath, setting forth to sail without oars.

Walking breeds holy forgetfulness. Holy forgetfulness can emerge in other ways as well: centering prayer at 5:30 a.m. in a special chair, matins at a monastery, practicing mindfulness in Zen meditation. But the walking pilgrim gradually leaves behind the distracted mind by physically leaving the spaces of those habitual distractions.

I'm not a Luddite. I took my phone on the Camino. I took pictures. In my bunk at night in the albergue, I sent text messages to my wife. When I had energy, I posted pictures with an update on my progress. Readers and friends encouraged me, even when my body was exhausted by the climbs, the distances, the weather.

That set of images and reflections on the journey, in part, have informed how I have now continued to use my digital devices. They are a model for how I'd want to reconstruct my relationship to the digital world. The steps I took were steps to real presence that provided a wisdom formed within my body, not outside of it.

The authentic pilgrim journey moves in two directions—outward and inward. The journey toward a holy destination enables us to cast off enough superficial layers to access our true selves. Many other contemplative practices also aid that. But I need to walk. The energy of walking dispels inner distractions. My steps accompany prayer, or, more likely, the quest just to be present. Gradually, my inner life drifts into focus.

The layers within, fashioned to protect access to our true, vulnerable selves, are not easily shed. Always, there is so much that we don't want to face. Once I was months and years into my contemplative journey, begun on that cold December day when I traveled to the monastery in Berryville, Virginia, my inward gaze slowly began to gain clarity. For instance, my irrational fear of binding commitments in life could no longer be hidden or explained away.

While at the monastery, I discovered Karen Horney's *Self-Analysis*. As I read her description of "Neurotic Self-Sufficiency," I felt as though I had been stripped naked, vulnerable, with no protective covering. I was facing my real self, more present than ever. Sometimes books are our first step before our feet begin the journey.

Carl Jung once wrote, "In my case Pilgrim's Progress consisted in my having to climb down a thousand ladders until I could reach out my hand to the little clod of earth that I am." The steps of the interior journey, however, need not end in endless cul-de-sacs of introspection. They also can lay bare unfathomable grace and love at the foundation of everything. At times unexpected, we sail into this ocean of love. It sweeps over us, maybe just for a moment, or for enough moments to remove the measurement of time. In such glimmering fragments of awe, we touch upon the real presence of God.

As Richard Rohr says, "Wisdom is not the result of mental effort." Our life's pilgrim journey proceeds by three movements that reach beyond the mind to the heart and the body: detachment, attention, and connection.

Detachment is the first step, already described. Beyond the incessant distractions delivered by our electronic screens, and the predictable comfort of normal routines and relationships, a pilgrim walks away for a time from the responsibilities of work or ministry. We detach ourselves from what we do to discover, or rediscover, how to be. I try to remember this: "Prayer is detachment from the fruit of our actions." That's what I sought, for instance, when moving cross-country from Washington, DC, to Missoula, Montana.

The pilgrim also becomes detached from their "self." Our culture preaches that everything revolves around the individual. The belief is that some version of the "self" is at the center, in control of our destiny. We speak the language of self-actualization, self-fulfillment, self-importance, self-sufficiency, and being a self-starter. Negatively, our disappointments, failures, and pains can become the sole lens through which we view all of life, again placing ourselves at the center. I don't discount the joy of achievement or the pain of our suffering. But seeing ourselves truly requires detachment from seeing ourselves at the center of everything. Detachment from intrinsic narcissism helps us become present to our true selves, dependent only on the mystery of God's breath. It's an inner freedom from the pressure of external expectations.

Detachment allows attention. For the Christian pilgrim, the individual is not walking away from an external world that is illusionary. Rather, they walk toward the deeper realities of God's presence, undergirding all that is. That requires a reflective, interior attentiveness. Detachment opens the space for this practice of the soul.

Images may be helpful, such as the boat without oars in the water, still guided by a wind, or a soldier at "attention," with a singular focus of one's body and mind, ready to hear and respond. Or antennae, which receive and transmit signals that move in a realm beyond sight and sound. The word *attend*, coming from the same root as *attention*, means a commitment to be present. All those images frame the picture and the practice of a pilgrimage.

Walking on a pilgrim's pathway provides a discipline for attention. At a physical level you can't be distracted from where your footsteps lead, for you may either slip and fall or lose your way. You also become more present to unexpected sights, like an ancient Celtic cross by a tree, or the words "Dios te habla, Dios te escucha," written as graffiti on a milepost: "God speaks to you, God listens to you."

You acquire presence toward what your pilgrimage presents on your way.

Attention allows connection. At some level, we all yearn to shed our false selves and become present to what mystics like Merton call our "true self." This is the core of our being, which rests apart from all that we do, which lies beyond all that we suffer, and which finds its life only in the flowing stream of God's love. That self is our truest identity, but it is hidden from us by all the layers of false selves, by all the distractions that divert our attention, and by all the voices that lure us away from the silence of presence.

A pilgrim's steps are inward movements seeking connection with their true self. Often on the Camino, I found myself asking, "Why are you who you are where you are?" But here's the mystery of encountering who we really are: in the contemplative journey of a pilgrim, this becomes linked to the experience of God's real presence. This presence is never anything that we attain. Instead, it is given, a pure, unexpected gift, outside of all control, but irreplaceable as the membrane surrounding our true self, our soul.

This intertwined connection to self and to God overflows in connection to others, and to all creation. The mystical irony is that pilgrim paths of solitude, when touching holy interior and exterior destinations, break forth into community. Attentive to the present, pilgrims meet one another eye to eye. Along the Camino, my continual surprise was how koinonia would erupt, in chance encounters anything but accidental. Real presence was not only my discovery of a truer self beyond the noise, in multiple moments; it was the experience of community with others.

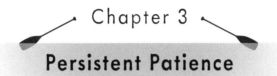

Chapter 3

Persistent Patience

Pilgrimage suggests a distance to be traveled, a terrain to overcome. And distance requires patience.

Anyone who has flown, taken a bus, driven a long distance knows the hum within a trip is "How soon will we arrive?" And any parent with a five-year-old in tow knows the plaintive cry from the back seat of the car, twenty minutes into a four-hour drive: "Are we there yet?"

It's difficult for children to wait. The brain must develop capacities for memory and attention span that make self-regulation possible. Eventually in the developmental process, patience becomes essential, requiring practice for a healthy control of impulses. For many, such learning can last a lifetime.

The famous "marshmallow experiment" at Stanford University in the 1960s claimed a link between a child's ability to control the urge for instant gratification and positive outcomes later in life. Children five to six years old were put in a room with a marshmallow (or another treat) on a table. They were told that if they waited, they could have two marshmallows, about fifteen minutes later. While the results of the test were instant, the subjects were then followed over several years. The long-term study showed that those who waited, and delayed gratification, were more likely to score higher on SAT tests, had better social skills, and were less likely to engage in substance abuse or to have eating disorders.

Several similar experiments refined and tested these results. This included researchers looking for other variables. More recent studies have indicated that young children today may have a slightly greater capacity to delay gratification than children fifty years ago—due in part to the prevalence of early childhood education programs. What remains clear from the research is that the development of patience is related to mature human development and emotional and psychological health.

Yet as a society we don't like to wait. That's not only related to speed of conveyance, which we looked at in chapter 1. The velocity factor is related to all areas of life: Goods of an unimaginable diversity are now accessible immediately to us with the click of a "buy" button. We are gratified. Amazon Prime provides free shipping to our doorstep in forty-eight hours.

Beyond consumerism, we're even rushing the regular processes of nature, where patience is not just a virtue but a necessity for growing plants and animals. Accelerated through various technological interventions, our foods are hastening toward us, while aspects of their development are making them less nourishing. Take the bioengineering of salmon. Canadian researchers perfected the ability to alter the DNA of salmon grown in fishery tanks, producing salmon about twice the normal size in half the time. Despite resistance by environmentalists, government regulators have allowed their introduction into the US market. Wild-caught salmon from Alaska may seem attractive, but the salmon fillet in your restaurant was likely bioengineered in a tank in Indiana.

Efficiency obliterates patience. We keep looking for the quick fix and rationalize extreme technological interventions to reduce waiting time not only in our foods, but in most every facet of our lives. Other societies not dominated by capitalistic market economies exhibit the opposite extreme. When visiting the Soviet Union before its collapse and traveling on the Trans-Siberian Railway across that vast country, in city after city I witnessed the same ongoing scene: people waiting in lines. For ordinary citizens, lines for groceries, medicines, buses, and vodka were a common reality. Delayed gratification was enforced by the inefficiency of their dogmatically held political and economic system. Ironically this became one of the major social complaints contributing to the weakening of Communist societies.

Yes, we know, intuitively, the basic lesson of the "marshmallow experiment": for anyone's healthy emotional development, the desire for instant gratification must be regulated. But learning the practices of patience within consumer societies is daunting. And it's not just about waiting for marshmallows. Or consumer goods. Some of life's most treasured gifts, like loving relationships, artistic skill, intellectual inquiry, and emotional healing, require patience.

One school for learning patience is pilgrimage. The desired endpoint may be weeks and miles and many footsteps away. It can't be rushed. You can only walk at about three miles an hour, and for some, even that is fast. Blisters, weather, and inadvertent detours can all intervene. And the pilgrim begins to see that gratification is redefined. *You will get there when you arrive*, the pilgrim learns. Patience liberates the one wandering for the love of God from the cult of efficiency, expanding those capacities to regulate the control of impulses—through memory and attention span. Our spiritual development requires those same capacities.

Early in his career, the Lutheran pastor Bill Thompson went to inner-city Baltimore to revitalize a struggling congregation. During his first sermon he played a recording of Willie Nelson's song "On the Road Again." The congregation wasn't quite ready for that. He told them, "Life is a spiritual journey," and that a prerequisite for setting out on any authentic spiritual journey was patience.

For a physical pilgrimage, patience becomes not only an act of the emotion or will but a practice that is embodied.

From my starting point in Ponferrada to Santiago de Compostela I walked 344,347 steps on the Camino. If asked at the start whether I could take that many steps, I wouldn't have known how to answer. I never imagined doing so. In my entire life, I had never walked fifteen miles in a single day. Taking those first steps, I couldn't really think of completing the whole pilgrimage. The only thing possible was to get on the path and patiently persist.

Even visualizing a day's goal seemed too far away to embrace. On our first day the four of us started at dawn out of Ponferrada in the shadows of its magnificent Templar Castle, found a café in a village for coffee, and passed through farmlands. After eight miles we entered vineyards in the Magaz Valley. Each place, each view, and each person revealed a fresh portrait. Roses blooming by the wall at the entrance to a home slowed and then stopped my steps. Trying to follow the small channels of ancient irrigation systems absorbed me, as did the focus on my steps. I couldn't think about the fact that we were only halfway to that day's anticipated destination.

But by about 3:30 we reached our intended albergue in Villafranca del Bierzo. We found available beds, among its seventy-seven, to accommodate the four of us. I checked to discover I had walked 42,256 steps. It didn't seem real, to finally arrive. And it seemed unthinkable that we would head out the next day before sunrise to again walk without the expectation of the day's end goal. What I *did* think of, at that point, was a shower, and then dinner, including a glass of Spanish wine. I discovered that the Camino asked for patience forged by careful attentiveness to the changing scenes and people coming directly before me, quieting the anxiety over whether and when we would reach our ultimate goal.

Before making the pilgrimage to Santiago de Compostela, "One step at a time" was a worn-out cliché. Now it became not only existentially true, but almost an epistemology for understanding the reality of those days. When I wasn't certain of anything else, I could be sure about taking another step. Patience in that setting was not some desired virtue, but the lubricant for each day's life.

The lessons may seem simple: desired goals in life, even when seeming completely out of reach, require our going step by step. Rushing the process often causes injury or means that the velocity cannot meet the long-term demands of the path.

The pilgrim's pace of one step at a time resonates with the rhythm of our soul. Our ultimate destination cannot be our daily focus. Rather, we open ourselves to each event, each person, each sorrow, each suffering, and each joy that we discover, daily, on our path. The spiritual wayfarer asks simply for the wisdom and the courage to take the next step. Sometimes that's all we can do. When we find a place of rest for our weary soul, we discover with amazement the thousands of steps we have traveled to that point.

Teresa Pasquale Mateus, writing in the Lenten devotional *Are We There Yet?*, shared from her time on the Camino de Santiago: "The walking is hard but also simple," she wrote. "One foot, then the next; deep breath in and deep breath out. . . . The everyday, in-your-own-place journey—the heart's navigation of life's obstacles—is the much harder path to tread."

Waiting for the second spiritual marshmallow goes against popular religious expectation. There is no veil between secular culture's focus on instant gratification and our religious culture's focus on spiritual gratification. It is, I believe, one of the damaging and unrecognized by-products of our frantic, market-driven, consumer economy that has bled over into every arena of our lives and turned religion into a consumerist venture. Millions turn to religion hoping for a quick fix and are disappointed, and then spiritually disillusioned.

Recall those walking forward at a Billy Graham rally. For them, it was a point of decision. But how many who walked forward were expecting an instant makeover of their lives? If they just gave their lives to Jesus, their marriages would be saved, their alcoholism would be ended, their lust would be erased, their gambling would cease, and their deceit would end. Their life's lack of purpose would be replaced with meaning and fulfillment. Their sorrow would turn to joy. The hold of sin over their lives would be broken. Their will would be empowered by God's Spirit.

I believe in conversion. I deeply rejoice in lives being transformed by a commitment to Jesus. It's just that the formula we're offered doesn't always honor the complexities, the long walk forward without knowing where it ends. Instant spiritual results are promised and anticipated. Billy Graham conducted evangelistic crusades in 417 different locations throughout the world, preaching to 215 million people. Tens of millions more heard him on radio and TV. At his crusades, about 2.2 million persons walked down the aisle, responding to Graham's invitation to accept Jesus. It's an astonishing story. But what happened to them?

Many studies have been done exploring that question, both by the Billy Graham Evangelistic Association and by outside research. The stories of those who testify to their lives being dramatically converted are legion and well documented. And Graham's method included trying to attach "inquirers"—those who came forward—to local congregations and provide them with some resources and publications. Yet research also shows that most of those coming to Graham's rallies were already involved in churches. Some friends of mine told me they went forward every time they attended a Graham rally. That it was like a Pavlovian response. And then there were the stories of those who walked down the aisle and, weeks or months later, walked away from the church and Christian faith. Those reports were also legion and require probing questions.

The evangelical subculture of the 1950s and '60s was my own, shaping my early life and faith. And the dominant belief was that any person could be dramatically and instantly transformed by a personal encounter with Jesus Christ. Such stories of famous converts formed an evangelical narrative that was soon iconography.

The vocabulary describing the narrative revealed prevailing assumptions. A convert who then began drifting into some former habits, who no longer was a regular attendee of church, was "backsliding." They were enjoined to be "victorious" over any ongoing temptations. The norm was a fervent relationship to Christ that regularly overcame any obstacles and kept the convert in a state of warm spiritual excitement. The description of the "dark night of the soul" as part of a person's faith journey was a foreign language, the language of mystics. Despite the popularity of John Bunyan's metaphorical book *The Pilgrim's Progress*, the idea of a physical pilgrimage as a spiritual practice was unthinkable. It was as though getting out of the chair to walk the aisles of the pavilion *was* the journey, when it was just the first steps.

When I was in my teens, most of my adolescent evangelical peers prayed most of the time about sex, which was seen as an obstacle to faith. A wrongly directed desire. Recently, I met with Tony and Peggy Campolo in Pennsylvania. Tony, a theologian and writer, decried the amount of energy and time evangelicals like him, me, and hundreds of thousands more spent agonizing in prayer over sex rather than other vital challenges of Christian discipleship. We couldn't focus on what the gospel required because we were fixated on keeping our sexual appetites under control. For those who were promised instant spiritual results, this was a problem that incorporated shame with our inability to avoid instant physical gratification.

Like all young adolescent boys, at some point I started to masturbate. I didn't even know the word, much less understand what was happening. And I was horrified, convinced that I was guilty of the most serious sin. Like all the young evangelical boys, I was also convinced that anyone with a real relationship with Jesus Christ would simply have the power to stop. The spiritual solution to this affliction would be immediate, lasting, and trustworthy. So I would pray—fervently and persistently.

On a calendar in my bedroom, I would make a mark on the date when I masturbated, convinced that this would be the last time in my life for such a vile act, and thanking God for the victory of the following days. Until the next "defeat."

In my sophomore year of Maine Township High School East, with its four thousand students, I ran for class vice president. I remember the day, coming in from track practice, when a girl from student council came running up to me to share the results that I had been elected. My first inner thought was, "Great. Now I'll never masturbate again." As a fine student, a campus leader, president of my church youth group, and president of the high school's Young Life Club, everyone thought I was a model of the perfect young adolescent Christian, including my parents. But not me. I was in inner psychological and spiritual agony.

In desperation and fear, I finally decided the one person I could go to and make my urgent confession was Bill Starr, my Young Life leader. With trepidation, I walked up the stairs of the Young Life office on Fairview Avenue in downtown Park Ridge, Illinois, closed the door, and started to share, clumsily. Bill got the picture immediately. He told me the name of this practice, explained how it was common, and assured me that my soul was not in danger. He then began to give me a picture of my Christian life, and my sexual self, that I'd never heard before. It didn't include easy answers or instant results. He told me that God's presence was with me, and that God wouldn't desert me. Think of this, he said, as an ongoing journey. He didn't use the word *pilgrimage*, but he described it. I walked down those stairs feeling as though I had recovered my young life.

The intense spiritual experience of conversion, or those pivotal turning points in a religious life, do not remain constant enough to sustain a lifelong spiritual journey. Our heart may be "strangely warmed," as the great founder of Methodism, John Wesley, wrote. But then it will cool. That's when the true test of our spirituality begins; that's where the steps go beyond the pavilion. But popular piety in books, in songs, and on radio and television refuses to acknowledge the absence of feelings, the dark night. And as such, it fails to issue the invitation to deeper faith.

Spiritual encounters in "thin space" can infuse life for brief, eternal moments with a sense of God's shimmering presence. This can grasp our inner being with transforming power in our pilgrimage. I know this. It's how I would try to describe a mystical experience at the Holy Cross Monastery in 1972. But I didn't remain in that state. Far from it. Yet memory has kept those moments alive. Memory has overcome my compulsion for instant spiritual gratification and nurtured patience, persistently. Memory reminds us of our story, and connects that story to God's story. We take this into ourselves at the Table, celebrating the life, death, and resurrection of Jesus, "in memory of me." These memories, patiently preserved in liturgical pageants, bid us to walk forward.

Such memory compels attention over a span of time. Attention span is the ability to "hold" our self for an ongoing period, focused on a certain reality. Spiritually this means holding a space open for our mysterious encounter with God's breath, or Spirit.

Attempts to hold one's spiritual attention have taken radical forms. In the Middle Ages, a movement grew for some Christians to leave normal society not by a pilgrimage, but by entering an extreme form of solitary life, seeking the experience of God through prayer, interceding for the world, and partaking in the Eucharist. They were called "anchorites," and they retreated into small cells, promising to live the rest of their lives in that place. This usually was a cubicle built onto the side of a church, with three windows—one into the church to receive the Eucharist, another to receive food, and a third to the outside to admit light, but with a cloth drapery.

This practice attracted more women than men—as high as four to one in the thirteenth century. One of the most famous, whose writings are with us today, was Julian of Norwich. Even though "anchorites"—men and women—adopted this radical form of physical withdrawal, the focused, inner spiritual attention of their lives made them sought after by those in the community. People would come to the window to ask advice, seek wisdom, and request guidance—including important persons of political influence.

These cells, or cubicles, were called "anchor-holds." In those confined spaces, their anchor held deep and their attention span long. In her wonderful account, *Pilgrim at Tinker Creek*, Annie Dillard is drawn to the same image to explain her experience:

> *I live by a creek, Tinker Creek, in a valley in Virginia's Blue Ridge. An anchorite's hermitage is called an anchorhold; some anchor-holds were simple sheds clamped to the side of a church like a barnacle or a rock. I think of this house clamped to the side of Tinker Creek as an anchor-hold. It holds me at anchor to the rock bottom of the creek itself and keeps me steadied in the current, as a sea anchor does, facing the stream of light pouring down.*

In the same time as anchorites, hundreds of thousands sought another way to focus their spiritual attention span by embarking on pilgrimage. Whether retreating into one stationary place or walking hundreds of miles away from familiar settings to a holy destination, the goal was the same—to hold the attention of their soul.

Leaving instant gratification behind is imperative for our pilgrim journey. This requires practices that cultivate memory and hold attention span, step by step, building persistent patience.

Chapter 4

The Strength to Let Go

For the pilgrim on the Camino, one of the first lessons in walking not only the first steps but the first steep incline is this: the pilgrim leaves behind anything that weighs us down.

My adventures with the backpack were constrained. Since trying to play football in high school, I've had a bad back. Now, with spondylolisthesis at the base of the spine, too much pressure or stress on my back quickly cripples my movements. I've tried many things to strengthen my core. In swimming exercise class, my instructor says fifty times in sixty minutes, "Belly button to the spine!" Strengthening core muscles stabilizes and protects the back. But I'm struggling against skeletal entropy.

Because carrying a heavy pack all day on the Camino de Santiago not only would have been a burden too heavy to bear but would have meant that even my walking would be impossible, I discovered that the Camino has an infrastructure in place to meet many individual practical needs. That includes JACOTRANS. The first early morning in

Ponferrada before heading out, I took an envelope provided by that enterprise, wrote my name and the intended destination, inserted a five-euro note, tied it to my backpack, and left it, walking away free—except for a day pack holding a liter of water, a rain parka, and whatever else was essential for the day. As if almost by magic, my new, lightweight backpack, purchased with investigative care from REI, was waiting for me when I arrived at the evening's destination.

In a way, this felt like cheating. What I unburdened myself of in the morning reappeared in the evening. But it also offered a physical way to help me reflect on leaving behind what weighed me down. And the irony wasn't lost on me: even our best efforts at relinquishment are only temporary. Even when they seem too much to bear, some burdens will stubbornly keep reappearing.

Most going on the Camino lay out possible items on a sofa for three weeks before leaving, trying to select what should fill the backpack. But once they start walking, too much baggage weighs them down. As I mentioned before, all manner of things are left along the way to lighten the load: shirts, extra shoes, towels, guidebooks, soap, socks, flashlights.

Pilgrims walk away from their lives to discover their souls. Those things that consume us with anxiety—our dissatisfaction with our work, worries about money, grief over our children's choices, tensions with those we most love, threats to our health—these usually, at their core, are afflictions from within. We need inward distance from their persistent, gnawing encroachments. These excess burdens on our psyche usually aren't solved until we first gain the inner detachment allowing us to set them down. Sometimes that inner detachment is aided by outward circumstances: a relationship crumbles, or best efforts fail to solve our biggest obstacles. But once we reach the place of inner detachment, the resolution comes more from relinquishment and trust than through struggle and angst. Relinquishment has its stages, as anyone on pilgrimage discovers.

Curiously the weight of what burdens us is lifted by our walking onward, rather than staying in place, obsessed with a cyclical search for solutions. When you walk long enough, you move into a holy mindfulness; memory is no longer an emotional prison, but a way to connect to moments that reach our core and strengthen it. Like a balm in Gilead, with the belly button to the spine.

In 1995 Bob Buford wrote *Halftime: From Success to Significance*. He wanted to show readers how they could achieve significant success and accomplishments in the first half of their lives, but then encounter a "halftime," when there's a break in the action. That's when they leave the playing field behind and move into another space to develop a new game plan. They emerge then on the field, ready to foster a commitment to deeper purpose, service, and spiritual fulfillment. Sports metaphors get used and ill used with great frequency. But this made sense to me. Buford's own journey led him to sell a prosperous TV broadcasting company and cofound the Leadership Network, a primary vehicle for supporting pastors of large, growing congregations.

With the initial success of his book, Buford founded the Halftime Institute. Through publications, coaching, and connections the institute focuses on those steps necessary for making a life-changing transition into one's second half of life. Buford's influence was widespread, strengthened by a partnership with management guru Peter Drucker.

The success of *Halftime* was certainly augmented by the language and metaphor of sports. Buford was from Texas, the land of Friday Night Lights, where football reigns supreme. Describing life as a football game resonated not only there, but in a country where the NFL now owns Sundays. Buford's subsequent books, including *Game Plan*, *Finishing Well*, and *Beyond Halftime*, continued to use sports as the metaphor to understand and evaluate one's life. And it was powerful. Stories attest to dramatic decisions redirecting energy and commitments of thousands in the second half of life.

Yet Buford was tapping into something more powerful than football. In the first half of life, ego strength needs to develop to provide the ability to define oneself as separate from external social pressures and expectations. Developing this "sense of self" means making decisions about what is perceived as good and bad, fostering a necessary separation of the ego as it shapes and protects one's emerging personhood. Youthful energy is then devoted to building skills, establishing discipline, and seeking social and economic success, as well as supporting family commitments. At this stage religion often plays a role as an external structure reinforcing standards of right and wrong, with a focus on doctrine and ritual, providing an outward system of reward and punishment.

I doubt that Bob Buford ever read much by Carl Jung. Jung explored how the psyche takes root in the first phase of the ego's development, pushing unwanted characteristics away in a necessary process of personality formation. However, these discarded dimensions then become part of one's shadow. In mature development, these must then be recognized and reintegrated, allowing the discovery of the true wholeness of one's self. Authors shaped by Jungian thought frequently write about the first and second halves of life, stressing the pathway of moving beyond the psychic restraints imposed in life's first phase to discover the true self, freed for generative love and spiritual meaning.

The journey into the second half of life is a pilgrimage. This is no automatic transition. Most, in fact, fail to take this step and remain confined in a life defined by the ego's accomplishments, guarded by external religious systems that "protect" and guarantee a sense of one's righteousness— imprisoning an identity dependent upon gratification from one's achievements. For Jung and for readers of the parables of Jesus, the grain of wheat, the ego, must die for the true self to emerge. The vulnerability and transparency necessary for this death require courage. At times this loss of ego can be terrifying.

The pilgrimage, then, embraces the leaving behind of the securities that the ego has developed over life's first half. The pathway is unknown, even if there are arrows to mark the way. Because it is untrodden ground for us, it can feel like we are walking naked into our future.

On the isolated pathway leaving Portomarin in Galicia, Spain, heading up a treeless hill, the August sun was unremitting. I walked alone and determined to press on. Eventually the Camino met up with a highway, accompanying it for what seemed endless kilometers. As I walked my solitude was interrupted by Jana, from Slovakia. Burned out after working on a start-up, she was between jobs and came on the Camino seeking renewal. Our conversation temporarily removed awareness of my depletion until we parted ways. Finally reaching a restaurant/bar for water and replenishment, I sat at a table near a Spanish man and his son, striking up a conversation. They asked how old I was and congratulated me on the kilometers I'd covered. But that exacerbated my worry. I still had kilometers to go, and the late afternoon only increased the sun's glare and heat. Picking back up, I headed along the way, and my steps slowed and began to falter. My Hanes "Cool Dri" polyester T-shirt was soaked through with sweat. It was another three kilometers to the aubergue where my companions were waiting.

I called a taxi.

Walking into the second half of life, at whatever age, can be like that.

Father Richard Rohr has written nearly fifty books, but by far the most popular has been *Falling Upward: A Spirituality for the Two Halves of Life*. First published in 2011, it has sold widely and worldwide. And while Buford sees the transition to the second half of life coming from a good half-time talk in the locker room, with hard work to follow, Rohr contends that this spiritual transition requires a loss of control, with experiences of emptiness, deconstructing the past systems of security and certainty. It's a pathway of lonely desolation. We walk away from the certainties undergirding who we have been, and we can't simply call a taxi.

In my own journey, and with those whom I've coached, mentored, or served as a spiritual director, *Falling Upward* is like a guidebook for our spiritual and psychological pilgrimages. Rohr makes sensible the systems of security that we construct in the first half of life. But with a certain psychic irony, the ego strength fostered by these systems becomes essential for leaving them behind, walking into liminal space with only hints of the wholeness and interconnection of life's second half. It takes strength to let go.

More than any other theologian, Rohr has made sense of Christ's crucifixion for me. Yes, I studied orthodoxy's magnificent emphasis on the cosmic victory of the cross and resurrection. I believed that deeply ever since reading *Christus Victor* in seminary, discovering the richness of Orthodox theology, with its icons of the resurrection, in my ecumenical experience. But Rohr emphasizes the vulnerable lack of control, leading to the abandonment, defeat, and desolation witnessed in the naked body of Jesus on the cross. This points to our own pathway for discovering the rebirth of our lives, beckoning us into a mystical union with Christ, and uniting us to all. This transition, following the way of the cross, is costly. When I now gaze at a crucifix in a Catholic church before illegally taking the Eucharist, I don't think of the doctrines of penal substitutionary atonement that I have rejected. Rather, I open my life again to the pathways of vulnerability and abandonment shown by my Lord, on the via dolorosa.

Introductions on the Camino are simple as strangers quickly become fellow pilgrims, companions on the Way. "Where are you from?" is the first question, almost always followed by, "Why are you on the Camino?" Lisa, from Oshkosh, Wisconsin, grew up with an unsatisfying mixture of Catholicism and Lutheranism. She's come alone, a spiritual searcher on the Camino. Clare is an extroverted Aussie from Melbourne. She works in HR and is between jobs. Days later I run into her again at Pilgrim's Mass in Santiago de Compostela, and her entire countenance is aglow. A man from Italy says he's been working with disabled people for twenty years and wanted a break. He's trying to take a bicycle on the Camino and now wants to come back in October. "Am I crazy?" he asks.

They ask me the same questions. I'm from the United States and live in Santa Fe, New Mexico. And then, sometimes I add, I'm a pastor, and the Camino has beckoned me. Things get stripped away on the Camino. I'd never say that I had been general secretary of the Reformed Church in America, which in any case would be incomprehensible to 95 percent of my fellow pilgrims. Nor would I say that I was an author, or that I had worked in the US Senate earlier in my career, or any of those things that had formed and defined me. That was baggage that I needed to drop off. On a pilgrimage you are just a pilgrim. And many are walking toward, or searching even subconsciously for, a second half for their lives.

These pathways are arduous. Rohr describes the system of securities that shape, form, and protect us in the first half of life as a "container." It holds our self together in ways that initially are necessary for our development. But then it needs to be dismantled, and in some cases shattered. Relinquishment becomes the spiritual coin of the realm as we enter this new psychic land. Yet this unlocks an astonishing inner freedom as the second half of life unfolds. Finding liberation from expectations driving what we ought to do, we discover the inner joy in doing those things intrinsically worth doing, following holy longings that awaken our soul.

James Hollis is a Jungian psychoanalyst and the author of *Finding Meaning in the Second Half of Life: How to Finally, Really Grow Up*. Hollis portrays the second half of life as offering the invitation to discover and root our lives in our soul. A question that can awaken that pilgrimage is, "Whose life am I living?" But as with other discerning guides, Hollis explores the fears, the potential loneliness, and the power of faulty ego securities and façades that so often impede those steps:

> *We need to be strong enough to examine our lives and make risky changes. A person strong enough to face the futilities of most desires, the distractions of most cultural values, who can give up trying to be adjusted to a neurotic culture, will find growth and purpose after all. The ego's highest task is to go beyond itself into service, service to what is really desired by the soul.*

The Camino changes pilgrims. For some it is dramatic: a fresh recovery of faith, a new journey free of imprisoning addiction, a redirection of one's vocational life, or the discovery of a living connection to one's soul and the inward presence of God. There may be others for whom the Camino is simply another experience, even something to put on one's résumé. But I have yet to encounter a pilgrim from the Camino who has not recalled that time as an exceptional space, where at least the portals to a life of deeper purpose, often in one's second half, have been opened like the majestic, ancient doors bidding pilgrims to enter the Cathedral of Santiago de Compostela.

Charles de Foucauld was born in Strasbourg, France, in 1858. Orphaned at age six, he was raised by his grandfather, who imparted to Charles faith as a Catholic. Eventually studies and experience shaping his development caused him to depart from religion. The death of his grandfather left him a rich financial inheritance. He joined the military, becoming an officer, and was sent to Algeria, a French colony. Captivated by the culture, and in conflict with his superiors over a romantic affair, he eventually resigned from the army and settled in Algiers.

Europeans were generally forbidden in neighboring Morocco. But undeterred, and leaving previous securities behind, Charles spent eleven months walking for 3,000 kilometers, or 1,800 miles, through that country disguised as a Moroccan Jewish rabbi. Returning to Paris, Christian faith became vividly alive for him, and he embarked on a pilgrimage to the Holy Land, spending Christmas 1888 in Holy Grotto of the Church of the Nativity in Bethlehem. Seeking an abandoned devotion to Christ, he became a Trappist Monk.

But Trappist stability couldn't contain Charles de Foucauld's wandering spirit. By 1901 he was back in Algeria, at Béni Abbès, committed to living a simple life among its inhabitants, striving to be in solidarity with the poor, and nurtured by the eucharistic presence of Jesus. Four years later he journeyed further into the heart of the Sahara desert, settling among the Tuareg people for more than a decade. Charles translated the gospels into the Tuareg language. His desire was to form a confraternity, or Catholic Order of those who would follow a witness of presence and solidarity amidst non-Christian peoples. His life was cut short when the effects of World War I reached Algeria. He was martyred by bandits connected to those fighting the colonizing French.

A pilgrimage marked by abandonment led Charles de Foucauld from comfort and wealth in Paris to poverty and vulnerability in the Sahara desert. He didn't plan this, but rather simply tried to follow, and kept moving forward, in consistent downward mobility with a radical faithfulness rarely witnessed. He had the strength to let go.

I first learned of his story when working on Capitol Hill and exploring life in the Church of the Saviour in Washington, DC. It was there I read Charles de Foucauld's Prayer of Abandonment:

Father,
I abandon myself into Your hands,
Do with me what you will.
Whatever you may do,
I thank you.
I am ready for all,
I accept all.
Let only Your Will be done in me,
and in all your creatures.
I wish no more than this, O Lord.
Into your hands I commend my soul
I offer it to you,

With all the love of my heart,
For I love you,
And so need to give myself,
To surrender myself into your hands
Without reserve,
And with boundless confidence,
For You are my Father.

This spirituality of abandonment is core to much of the contemplative tradition. On retreats at Trappist monasteries, this message resonated within me. Of course, Charles de Foucauld's example is striking because it is so extreme. Not every journey into one's second half of life ends up in a remote desert. But walking away from false securities does become a prerequisite when we cast off into a life of pilgrimage. Those false securities weigh us down in ways not fully realized until we begin to shed them. Take heart; this courageous and painful way of abandonment, faithfully followed, yields a surprising lightness of being. We can walk further, with steps that are now truly our own, leading to a future abandoned to God.

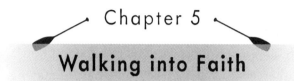

Chapter 5

Walking into Faith

The journey of one hundred thousand pilgrims to Tabieorar is hard to describe. Many come because it is their church's annual gathering event connecting them to one another, providing a group identity in a society permeated by various divisions. Some come out of a genuine thirst for a spiritual blessing and material promise that will help sustain them in daily lives marked by marginalization, where employment is as uncertain as the weather, and the price of rice in this food-deficit nation is a barometer of livability.

But thousands upon thousands come. They began arriving in the afternoon at Mount Tabieorar, a dusty, expansive space about thirty-five miles outside of Lagos, Nigeria. Pilgrims from throughout the country made their way to the festival, held annually for the eighty-third time, on land considered sacred.

They settled in, with frayed tarps, blankets, bottles of water, and thin white plastic bags like those provided at home by Walgreens, filled with bread, fruit, and other meager rations. Vendors selling wares stood outside the entrances, with candy bars, bananas, and other treats piled on trays balanced gracefully on the heads of women. The vendors with mobile propane stoves cooked hot foods. The festive atmosphere had the feel of a Nigerian tailgate party, without the cars and SUVs. But it was holy.

At 8:00 p.m. our hosts arrived at the guest house where three other ecumenical guests and I were staying. They gave each of us a white robe, made especially for us. The Church of the Lord (Aladura), host of the Tabieorar Festival, is one of Africa's churches where all worshippers wear white robes, symbolic of their baptismal cleansing. We arrived at the festival in our white garments and our bare feet. Like Moses at the burning bush and Joshua at Jericho, God's presence at this particular place made it holy ground, requiring humility expressed through removing one's sandals.

Tens of thousands of shoeless saints robed in white swayed and danced as they sang and prayed, long into the night. The sermon from Archbishop and Primate Rufus Ositelu began at 1:00 a.m., focused on the "God of Possibilities." More corporate prayers for needs and blessings followed, until 4:00 a.m.

I was caught up in the embodied joy of this church. These pilgrims were hungry for a faith that is tangible, embodied, and experiential—a faith that captivates body and their soul. At 2:30 a.m. they still found the energy to rise and dance. Some privileged enough to have plastic chairs near the front of this endless mass of worshippers may have sat and dozed for a while, but a fresh song and resounding music jolted them again out of their chairs to absorb more of the spiritual energy that seemed to blow through the night on Mount Tabieorar. All were seeking an expression of religious faith that would pour and pulsate through their veins.

After a day of confused sleep, I traveled from my hotel by Lagos's Murtala Mohammed International Airport back to Ogere Remo to visit the modest headquarters of the Church of the Lord Aladura. Smiling faces greeted me in cramped, cluttered offices with desks piled high with folders and papers as ceiling fans slowly turned. Either I was an hour early or Archbishop and Primate Ositelu was an hour late for our appointed meeting; that didn't matter to anyone. Another archbishop and deputy graciously welcomed me, with this unplanned interruption received as an occasion for hospitality.

The conversation turned to my reactions to the Tabieorar Festival.

"In my church tradition, and many in the West," I offered, "we tend to keep our faith centered in our heads."

The archbishop chuckled. "We believe," he responded, "that our faith has to move through every part of our body."

The pilgrims coming to Mount Tabieorar came to embody their experience of God, carrying them through the night and into the days and nights that would follow. They came to a holy place, discovering a holy space, and put bare feet to the ground, reaching their whole self, robed in white, and dancing their way into faith.

The temptation left by the Reformation is to think our way into faith. In my tradition I've never been invited to dance my way into faith. My faith journey and the denomination I served, the Reformed Church in America, is rooted firmly and deeply in the Reformation. The startling accomplishments of this historic movement hardly need to be recounted. Theological pioneers displayed indefatigable courage in defying centuries of ecclesiastical power and tradition. The stench of prelacy and papal corruption was met with fierce resistance. Groundbreaking doctrines rooted truth in biblical revelation and founded salvation on promiscuous grace.

Christiansfeld, Denmark, was founded in 1773 as a colony and planned town for Moravian believers. The Moravian Church moved within streams of the Reformation, but with its own private history and somewhat cloistered identity stressing simplicity and the life of prayer.

Today the Moravian congregation in the center of Christiansfeld has about 180 members in the town of 3,000. The church building is striking in its sheer simplicity. As its pastor, Dr. Jorgen Boytler, explained, the interior is completely plain, with no pictures, images, paintings, stained glass, or symbolic representation of any kind. There's no altar, and not even a pulpit—only a speaking table, with a podium and chair by the wall at the center of the worship space. Wooden benches painted white, amidst gray walls, provide the seating. Simple chandeliers, each holding four real candles, help illumine the space, although some electric lighting has been added. Nowhere is there even a cross on display.

The worship service was entirely from the Danish Moravian Prayer Book, which includes Lutheran liturgy as well as hymns by the famous Danish pastor, poet, and philosopher Grundtvig and liturgy specific to the Moravians. The only physical movement was when the congregation stood, and then sat. The pastor read a thoughtfully prepared sermon.

This worship service focused on words and thoughts, conveyed with rational care and intentionally restrained emotion. It stayed in the head. And the lack of any symbolic, artistic décor on walls that were plaintively blank meant there was no visible distraction from the spoken and sung words.

The worship building and service in the heart of Christiansfeld reflected a broad stream of the Reformation that reached into northern Europe and then to the British Isles. For most, specific creeds and confessions particular to their denominational tradition became credentials of "true faith" and excluded those who thought and believed differently. As versions of the true faith continually multiplied, expressions of the church endlessly divided. Religious faith became centered on what one believed, and how one thought.

The distance from the Tabieorar Festival in Nigeria was not just historical and geographical; the tens of thousands gathered all night on that holy ground represented a wholly different way of appropriating and practicing Christian faith.

Pilgrims walk, or dance, their way into faith.

The Way is made by walking. Not simply by thinking our way into dogmatic creeds.

Because of the pressure to dogmatize convictions that rejected prevailing dogma, the Reformation rushed to formulate secure intellectual declarations of the tradition's beliefs, called Confessions. It was its defense mechanism. First was Luther, beginning with the Large and Small Catechisms, and then the Augsburg Confession, written by his colleague Philip Melanchthon in 1530. But as the Reformation splintered, more followed. Between 1520 to 1650, around forty to fifty "definitive" Confessions were written. For Presbyterians this culminated with the Westminster Confession of Faith, the Larger and Shorter Catechisms, the Directory of Public Worship, and the Form of Church Government.

Confessions are intended to formulate the right theology about God and the church. This assumes that faith, as I said, is formed by thinking our way into it. And while many of my Protestant colleagues may protest that last sentence, it's where the weight of historical practice has fallen.

The Reformed Church in America had three historic Confessions, or "Standards of Unity," for most of its history: the Belgic Confession (1561), the Heidelberg Catechism (1563), and the Canons of Dort (1619). In 2010 the RCA added the Belhar Confession, which emerged out of the struggle of churches in South Africa against apartheid. But most beloved is the Heidelberg Catechism, consisting of 129 questions and answers, divided into fifty-two "Lord's Days," so that it could be taught one Sunday each week for a year.

Other Protestant traditions cling to their specific Confessions. Correctly formulating faith was not just about differing opinions. Beliefs had life-and-death consequences, foremost between Catholics and Protestants. During France's Wars of Religion, an estimated two million people perished. The Thirty Years' War in central Europe, fomented by this religious division, eventually killed eight million. But conflicts among Protestants also ensued, with Reformed and Lutheran persecution of Anabaptists. Both the Augsburg Confession and the Belgic Confession condemn them, and Luther urged their execution as heretics. Thousands of Anabaptists became martyrs.

The Reformation's addiction to getting theological ideas precisely right, in ways that often conflicted with other Protestants, placed the stress on preaching the right words as well as teaching the right ideas. Pure doctrine rightly proclaimed put the pulpit at the center, or high and lifted up on a pillar.

The journey of faith became immobilized and disembodied. Getting the propositional formulations of faith right, with their life-and-death consequences, was what really mattered. Confessions became the containers for the correct words about faith; enclosed and protected, it was faith in a box. Scottish poet Edwin Muir, in his poem "The Incarnate One," puts it succinctly: "The Word-made-flesh here is made word again."

In the thinking of the Reformation, pilgrimages were not only considered unnecessary; they were considered part of the system of spiritual superstitions being overthrown, with their relics, saints, and supernatural transformation of elements in the natural world—even, for some, bread and wine. Embodiment was suspect. John Calvin, in the words of author Julie Canlis, worried about the "base fusing of the physical with the spiritual" that pilgrimages encouraged, leading to idolatry. Martin Luther in typical fashion put it bluntly: "All pilgrimages should be stopped. There is no good in them; no commandment enjoins them, no obedience attaches to them."

Stop walking. Keep thinking, to avoid heresy and idolatry.

I'm walking out of my confessional box.

My pilgrim's progress finds me walking away from attempts to corral my faith, to declare that this and not that is how we must understand the word of God, and how we must understand God.

Before I was ordained as a "Minister of Word and Sacrament," I underwent examinations by the Holland Classis. *Classis*, comprised of a group of congregations, is a Latin term originally referring to a fleet of ships—not to be confused with ships without oars. The examinations were led by Ministers of Word and Sacrament and Elders, who constitute a shared governing body. The Classis controls ordination, and members of the Classis wanted to know if I was fit.

I was asked by one leading pastor if I had any reservations about the statements in the RCA's Confessions.

I replied, "Well, I don't believe in drowning Anabaptists." It was a smart-ass comment, ill considered. Ulrich Zwingli, a leader of the Reformation, sanctioned the drowning of Frederick Manz, an early Anabaptist, in the Limmat River at Zurich, Switzerland, on January 7, 1527.

I stood before the Classis at historic Third Reformed Church in Holland, Michigan, on June 10, 1984, wearing a white robe but with shoes, answering the liturgical questions posed to every person at ordination and reading the Form of Declaration, which includes this sentence: "I accept the Standards [meaning our Confessions] as historic and faithful witnesses to the Word of God." Members of the Classis laid hands on me, and I was ordained.

Today, I couldn't make that same declaration with a clear conscience. Though I would likely make the same smartass comment. That's not the point. I'm no longer willing to force my faith into neat confessional boxes, declaring this is the only way to understand the word of God.

So, I'm leaving those Confessions behind. They are like oars that at one point were essential to guide fleets of floundering boats in the stormy seas of sixteenth- and seventeenth-century Europe and providing a safe theological harbor. But now they hinder the journey, even pushing against the wind of the Spirit.

For fellow pilgrims carrying similar baggage, let me say I believe that how we think about God, of course, does matter. Faith is about more than feelings. Giving shape, expression, and intellectual coherence to the spiritual journey, and to God's place in the whole cosmos, is a continuous, essential calling. Yet I also know that many in various faith communities and I have gotten things backwards for a long time. We haven't walked. We haven't danced.

The historically complex combination of the Reformation and the Enlightenment pushed Christianity to encapsulate the mystery of faith into abstract, coherent intellectual systems. Those came to function as the gateways and guardrails that were supposed to lead the individual into faith and keep them there. But the physical world was forgotten. Heads were severed from bodies.

Some sought the recovery of inner spiritual experience as the focus of faith. In doing so, religious belief too readily became privatized, and Christian faith merged with the American experiment, in which Christianity was captured by individualism. This time the heart, instead of the head, was detached from the body. Inward, existential spiritual realities were in a realm separated from the material world.

Embodied experience connects the head and heart with the entirety of ourselves. Walking on a pilgrimage connects the physical and the spiritual. Faith burns in that crucible.

As I walked further on the Camino to Melide, where two ancient routes of the Camino join before the final fifty kilometers to Santiago de Compostela, I was exhausted. I was behind my companions, as usual, going at the pace of my artificial knees. Prayer was halting. Each step a challenge. But fellow pilgrims I encountered inspired me, walking next to me or walking past with a kind word. I met a Spanish family with three young children, all walking the Camino together. Finally trekking up the hill I found the municipal center and collapsed in a bed, sleeping before supper.

That evening, reunited with Kyle, Mark, and David, we found a restaurant featuring the region's speciality, *pulpo a feira*—boiled octopus. Accompanied by bread and red wine, we feasted, shared, and reflected on our journeys—both that day's and our lifetimes'. It was eucharistic. We were feasting our way into faith.

When you walk, when you feast your way into faith, when you dance on holy ground, things shift. You reflect differently. You approach God differently. As my steps on the Camino and steps to live an embodied faith have moved me, things have changed.

I've come to doubt my belief in beliefs.

The Zurich city council, which had converted to Reformed faith and enforced it, condemned twenty-nine-year-old Felix Manz to drowning for his belief in adult rebaptism. He was taken in a boat, with his hands tied, to the center of the river. An associate of Zwingli was in the boat, still urging Manz to "convert." They believed that when Manz was drowned, he would go to hell. But if he changed his mind and said he no longer believed in rebaptism for adults awakened to faith, then his salvation would be restored. Who today, of those who follow Jesus, believes that could be true?

This belief in beliefs pervades strands of Christianity. In the ruins of Philippi, in today's Greece, I've looked into a cave said to be the jail where Paul and Silas were imprisoned and miraculously freed at midnight. As the story is told in the book of Acts, the jailer was about to kill himself, and Paul restrained him. "What must I do to be saved?" the jailer asked. "Believe in the Lord Jesus Christ, and you will be saved," Paul and Silas replied.

I heard that verse a thousand times, torn out of context, used as proof text, and I believed it formed the core of the gospel. But what it came to mean was another box: believing a set of theological propositions about Jesus that granted a person eternal salvation.

Confessions contained the content for right belief. Right belief gets elaborated in how we think about God and the Bible and, by extension, the role of leaders, acts of justice, women in leadership, same-gender relationships, and more.

In the story about Paul and Silas, New Testament scholars point to how "believing" in that story and throughout the account of the emerging church does not mean intellectual assent to a set of propositions.

"Faith" is different from belief. It's an event. And faith is made by walking. For me the question seems simple. How is a person to hold to the belief that when they tipped the boat to plunge Felix Manz into the Lammat River, he was descending to hell? Or that Ulrich Zwingli's salvation was guaranteed by his correct Reformed beliefs?

Within those containers, there is no room for those who walk. There is no room for Manz's embodied practices of simple discipleship and sharing goods in community.

Pilgrimage tells a different story about faith because it focuses on practices, on where we walk, what we see, how we greet, whether we share, whom we trust, and how we are led. Abstract belief systems get deconstructed through countless steady steps keeping our feet, our hearts, and our minds to the ground, grounded.

And faith traditions aren't the only containers. We have beliefs about how our economic system should function, about what political party is the container for truth, about what sets of behaviors are acceptable or not. With or without religion, we amass containers as a form of controlling our lives.

This isn't just about theology. We bring these fixed ways of seeing the world, or doing our business, or relating to our neighbors, or planning our retirement, that are based on enclosed, secure containers, keeping things clear, black and white. But that's what can inhibit us and forestall real openings for growth and new life. We remain comfortable with what we can predict, understand, and control, including controlling others. It requires a step out of those boxes, involving risk, but entering a terrain where new avenues can be discovered.

A path of pilgrimage challenges us all to step free.

The way of the pilgrim is the long path. It is dancing our way into faith, or feasting our way into faith, and certainly walking our way into faith.

Chapter 6

Reckless Spirituality

Taylor Holbrook arrived from Ghost Ranch, New Mexico, at the Atrisco Café in Santa Fe to have dinner. He chose the evening's special, a pork chop smothered in beans and cheese with red and green chile. A lamb burrito was fine for me. The nourishment came from the conversation.

Holbrook had been a "successful" pastor, revitalizing a slumbering, historic congregation into a thriving ministry. Over two decades, his winsome style, gifted preaching, and commitment to social outreach drew scores of members, and he built a model for how congregations could have a resonant witness in local communities and the larger public square.

But Taylor was always theologically curious, open, and growing. When his niece came out as gay and was married, it impacted Taylor, whose views were already evolving in a more inclusive direction. He began trying to nudge the congregation toward an open and affirming view of LGBTQ persons. Taylor wondered whether the constraints of his orthodoxy could respond to the questions outside voices were addressing about the relevance of Christian faith.

And he began to question whether the domesticated, entrenched structures of the organized church in America could convey a future message of faith with any enduring power in a rapidly changing, secularized culture.

With the option of an early retirement, Taylor stepped away from this flourishing ministry and walked forward in his pilgrimage. Over dinner he told me about his time at Ghost Ranch. He had just attended a session of the Seminary of the Wild, titled "Wild Christ, Wild Earth, Wild Self." The main speakers were Richard Rohr and Geneen Haugen, but the session wasn't just about listening and note taking. As an introduction to the seminary's life and program, it was "an experiential, nature-based journey of apprenticeship into the wild mysteries of the Kingdom of God." As its description explained, "Finding a way forward for the Pilgrim, the Church, and the Culture will require that we live in alignment with the life-enhancing wisdom of Creation."

Taylor spent time in practices designed to attune his soul to the earth, connect with the Holy, and discover his unique calling in an interconnected world. On a solitary hike into the red rock mountains, he came to a large stagnant pool. Below, some clear water was flowing.

"For me, I saw that as the organized church," Taylor explained. "It's lost its life, trapped in putrid patterns of stagnation. I'd like to smash and remove rocks below and free some flowing water." New, fresh, liberating forms of church had to break forth, requiring old structures to die.

Brian Stafford is one of the cofounders of the Seminary of the Wild. A graduate of evangelical Wheaton College, Stafford went on to hold an endowed chair in psychiatry before walking away from academia to "serve the deeper mysteries of the world and the psyche." He's now a guide, mentor, writer, and poet, working with others in the Seminary of the Wild with its goal of "Embodying the Journey of the Wild Christ to Renew the World." This consists of a blend of ecotheology and an experiential connection to the sacredness of creation, rediscovering its essential "wild" reality long subdued, boxed in, and domesticated by modern culture and religion. Within this, the individual reconnects to the purpose of their soul.

The Seminary of the Wild was tame for Taylor Holbrook as he began to cast off oars in his pilgrimage. Other spiritual adventures included the Animas Valley Institute, leading him and others on an inner quest at California's Joshua Tree National Park in a "Soulcraft Intensive" experience. Practices Animas's facilitators use in these intensives include "Deep Imagery Work with Animal Guides," "Talking across Species Boundaries," and "Befriending the Dark."

The Animas Valley Institute was founded in 1981 by Bill Plotkin, a psychologist and wilderness guide who has guided thousands on "pancultural vision quests." Plotkin has written major works, including *Nature and the Human Soul: Cultivating Wholeness and Community in a Fragmented*

World and *Soulcraft: Crossing into the Mysteries of Nature and Psyche*. Animas and the Seminary of the Wild are influenced by Thomas Berry, the Catholic priest who pioneered in ecospirituality, telling "the story of the universe," and other developers of ecotheology.

Taylor is joined on this journey by hundreds of thousands today who are seeking forms of spirituality that rediscover and restore the intrinsic connection between humanity and the material creation. These take wildly diverse expressions. Some move in terrain that is beyond the confines of established, major religious traditions, although frequently drawing on forms of indigenous spirituality practiced by native peoples. Other expressions work within the broad framework of the Christian tradition, rediscovering biblical themes of God's interwoven, sacred connection to creation and all humanity and recovering forms of spiritual practice that embody that grounded reality.

Christian approaches to unearthing God's shimmering presence in the material realities of air, earth, fire, and water, sustaining all life, often focus obsessively on the incarnation. Our modern Enlightenment portrayal of the world is "excarnate." Embodied practices of spirituality and faith where physical, material reality is enlivened through the holy presence of God's Spirit are essential rebellions against modernity's supposed norms. Pilgrimages are one such form of rebellious, embodied spirituality.

These various forms of spiritual practice, whether in soul quests through the wilderness or casting off in a tiny boat without oars into the sea, seem reckless. They appear untethered to orthodoxy and to rationality because they are tethered to the earth, and to the Spirit.

Why do they seem spiritually reckless and wild? Perhaps because our inherited, habitual forms of spiritual practice have been domesticated and tamed.

The incarnation was the final, divine assault on the belief that the material world was only matter and didn't matter. It is, for Christians, the most reckless, wild act of God. Certainly, it opens pathways for a reckless spirituality that is tethered to faith in an incarnate, rather than an excarnate, world—always, ever infused with God's presence.

Pilgrims move in two directions at the same time—an outward direction toward a holy destination and an inward journey seeking an encounter with the sacred. Two of the best academic scholars of pilgrimages, Victor and Edith Turner, explain it in this one sentence: "Pilgrimage may be thought of as extroverted mysticism, just as mysticism is introverted pilgrimage." Pilgrimages, they suggest, were, and are, no walk in the park, or plain, or mountain. Embarking on such a journey, we become untethered not just from our physical normalcy. These uncertain, trusting steps also move us out of our spiritual familiarity. The pilgrim is invited not only to walk out of boxes of dogmatic beliefs, but also to walk away from practices of comfortable spirituality.

Consider historically the life of peasants or serfs in medieval Europe who were tied to specific places—a manor, and a particular piece of land. Religious life was likewise confined to a local parish, with its repeated, routine practices. As pilgrimage opportunities began to be possible for a wide range of people, their journeys liberated them toward places unknown, with spiritual intensity. Pilgrimage sites were places where miracles had occurred. The bones of saints were living; the apparition of Mary created a rarified space. Healings occurred, continuing the miraculous nature of these sites.

As journeys to Jerusalem became insurmountable or impossible, numerous pilgrimage sites sprang forth throughout Europe. Yet those embarking on pilgrimages faced clear and present dangers. They were walking into liminal space, with a familiar past of place and spirit left behind and a future promise of spiritual power, wedded to tangible, material things, in the distance.

In their own context, this was a reckless spirituality, a form of extroverted mysticism. Of course, the underbelly of pilgrimage motives can't be ignored—those seeking indulgences, or paid to travel on behalf of a wealthy, sedentary sinner, or those sentenced to a pilgrimage as recompense for a crime. But for most, this was a once-in-a-lifetime embodied quest of spiritual abandonment. In the words of the Turners, "pilgrimage was the great liminal experience of the religious life."

For today's pilgrim it can be the same. A pilgrimage is a rejection of modernity's expectations and assumptions about time, place, perception, satisfaction, speed, predictability, and the material world. As in ancient times, motives for contemporary pilgrimages are mixed. Lines between pilgrimage and tourism become blurred for some while breaks in employment prompt others to a pilgrimage more than a thirst for embodied forms of holiness. Yet pathways that move simultaneously in inward and outward directions prove irresistible to throngs roaming pilgrimage paths today.

The most popular guide to the Camino de Santiago is written by John Brierley. It's the closest thing to a Bible that many pilgrims carry. Brierley breaks the Camino into segments that can be walked each day (though many dispute his assumptions about distance and endurance). The villages and sites are carefully recounted, with suggestions for pilgrim lodging and food.

Starting each of these thirty-three stages he recounts "the practical path" and then "the mystical path." For instance, going from Molinaseca to Villafranca del Bierzo, reflecting on the story of the Templar Castle's ruins in Ponferrada, he asks, "Are we ready for a leap of faith, ready to withdraw our investments in the limited consensual reality and bank instead on Reality unlimited?" Such interrogation of the soul, prompted by the places, shrines, and thousand-year-old stories of the Camino, confront the cloistered, secure patterns of spirituality that the pilgrim brings to the journey and can learn to leave behind. Again, to quote *Image and Pilgrimage in Christian Culture*:

A pilgrim is one who divests himself of the mundane con-comitants of religion—which become entangled with its practice in the local situation—to confront in a special, "far" milieu, the basic elements and structures of his faith in their unshielded, virgin radiance.

In my experience, mysticism has always involved movement. That's not like the unique whirling dervishes' mystical prayers practiced for seven hundred years by the Sufi branch of Islam, although that is a fascinating study. Rather, simply walking, mindful of God's presence, helps walk me away from inherited forms of spiritual practice.

My previous acts of faith devotion included almost solely reading a passage of Scripture and silently praying, generally asking God to do certain things. What is changed by walking is focus. My focus is on presence—beginning regularly with the simple attempt to bring my inner self present to the reality of God's love, which already and always is there, in each breath, and each step, upholding my life.

In one way or another, the Spirit yearns to break out and to break open our old practices, our protective shells of comfortable spirituality, connecting our inner selves more deeply to God's love and to God's world. Your soul no longer stays still. It's moving with God in the world, and moving toward God, revealed in signs or shrines or saints or surroundings. The pilgrim's walking body holds incarnate this inner journey of the soul, often recklessly.

The Holy Spirit is the wild card in the Trinity. God the Father is discernable, almost understandable, though often formidable. The Son is seen in the incarnation's mystery, tangible in flesh and blood, but cosmic in an eternal, redeeming presence. But what of the Spirit? Described by the Nicene Creed as the "giver of life," present in the beginning as the breath of God, poured out in explosive power to form the church, prompting the deepest sighs of human hearts while groaning with the travail of all creation—this is the unpredictable, energizing, even reckless component of the Trinity's life.

This recklessness of the Spirit keeps disrupting normal practices of spirituality, religion, and culture. At the bizarre eruption of the Spirit at Pentecost described in the book of Acts, Parthians, Medes, Elamites, plus those living in Mesopotamia, Judea, Cappadocia, Pontus and Asia, Phrygia and Pamphylia, along with Cretans and Arabs all suddenly understand one another's incomprehensible native languages with tongues of fire. The Spirit is never captured by settled and secure boundaries of language and culture.

That pattern continues as the journalistic story of Acts unfolds. The preaching of Peter and Stephen encountered opposition in Jerusalem in part because it proclaimed that God's compassion, revealed in Jesus, reached out to all those in need of reconciliation, rather than being limited to a closed circle claiming an exclusive monopoly on God's holiness. Stephen paid with his life for this testimony.

This message became embodied in the movement of those who proclaimed it. Philip took the message to

Samaria—despite the historic hostility between the Jews and the Samaritans. Then, incredibly enough, an angel of the Lord told Philip to journey south, toward Gaza and the wilderness. There he encounters the Ethiopian eunuch. He is a foreigner, a gentile, and, as a eunuch, a person with an ambiguous sexuality. He was explicitly prohibited from worshipping at the temple, even though he had made a pilgrimage to Jerusalem. But this Spirit demolishes those stern lines of division and protected practices of spirituality. And Philip baptized the Ethiopian eunuch—bringing the body to water and sacralizing both. This story unlocked for me how I meet those excluded from the church because of their sexuality. It shows how the Spirit guides the boat without oars, giving someone without a faith community a community. Offering encounter, being met by Philip as he is.

The story of this unpredictable, uncontrollable Spirit continues as Peter receives a vision at Joppa, being told to eat what he thought was unclean and thereby destroying his well-ordered religious practices that always separated Jew and gentile. He then is brought to Cornelius, a Roman soldier, and his household, to whom Peter now declares that "God shows no partiality." Then, to the astonishment of those with Peter, the same Holy Spirit is poured out on those hearing this message in what is sometimes called the Gentile Pentecost. Peter's response is to say, "Who am I, that I should hinder God?"

All this sets the stage for the story of the Church at Antioch. Many early followers of Jesus fled Jerusalem, and some traveled as far as Antioch, walking twice as far as my ten-day journey from Ponferrada to Santiago de Compostela. Unlike Jerusalem, the center of Judaism with no more than fifty thousand people, Antioch was the third largest city in the Roman Empire, with between five hundred thousand and eight hundred thousand inhabitants. This population was highly multicultural, with Syrians, Cypriots, Egyptians, and Persians, along with many others, who had migrated there. About one-third of those in this city were slaves.

Here in Antioch the young church grew and flourished as a multiracial, multicultural community. Its leaders included Simeon, also called Niger, a black African gentile, as well as Manaen, who was from the court of the Jewish king Herod. The "headquarters" in Jerusalem was anxious about this unorthodox new church breaking comfortable boundaries of religious practice. But Jerusalem's envoy, Barnabas, rejoiced in the liberating power of the Spirit he found there, eventually becoming one of its leaders.

Barnabas then went to find Saul, the converted former persecutor of those who followed Jesus, now named Paul, and brought him to this newly created church in Antioch. And what happened? As they fasted and prayed, they discovered that the Holy Spirit was calling them to join God's mission in the world. Sent out by the Spirit, Paul and Barnabas embarked on the first of these "missionary journeys," not unlike those Celtic pilgrims casting off without oars. All this started from an upstart church in Antioch, and in three centuries the known world was transformed. And for all of this to happen, those early, fearful pilgrims had to walk away from Jerusalem.

The work of this hyperactive Spirit continually breaks out in embodied ways. We're told of physical healings, vivid visions, and a spoken, enraptured language of praise. Those untouched, then and now, frequently dismiss such manifestations of the Spirit as esoteric, primitive, delusional spirituality, if not worse. But for those participating in this empowerment, their bodies and the material world are reconnected to a life-giving spiritual presence. Further, when fully experienced, community is created.

To step forth into a liberating pilgrimage, we don't have to desert the Bible for a journey into an unknown wilderness area with the wild hope of communing with trees, although that's a worthy option. An alternative is to simply read the Bible, with these stories of a wild, liberating Spirit. They describe and call for embodiment.

Theologians who try to describe the indescribable, like the nature of the Trinity, are fond of suggesting that the Holy Spirit is the love that flows between the Father and the Son. Maybe that's what defines the Spirit's recklessness, for that love can't be restrained from breaking out into all that God has created.

The church's creeds, confessions, polity, and denominational structures, which keep evolving, seem like anxious attempts to make sense of and control the Spirit's continual disruption of established forms and understandings. Outbreaks of the Spirit in revivals, renewals, and Reformations create an understandable impulse to recodify and restructure life together.

All this, however, depends on the courage to walk forward through embodied, reckless forms of spirituality, leaving our Jerusalems behind in a pilgrim journey of restless faith, grounded in a love fueled by Trinitarian mysteries.

Chapter 7

Unpredictable Grace

Jim Knol set off with a companion for a ten-day pilgrimage on the Camino de Santiago. For twenty-seven years, Jim had served at the Christian Health Care Center in Wyckoff, New Jersey, completing a remarkable career as director of pastoral care and earning a lifetime achievement award for his work in the field of aging. This would be an achievement of a different kind. And it required walking. As he and his companion walked they encountered two other pilgrims. The women shared excitedly about how they had thoroughly planned each aspect of their journey, making reservations ahead for where to stay at each night of their carefully calibrated walk. As the two women walked on, Jim and his companion reflected. That was no way, in their view, to do a pilgrimage. It missed the whole point.

Their path may be plotted but is never predictable, thought Jim. The truth is pilgrims lose control. Their way is intended to be open. Relinquishing their control, step by step, becomes one of their most remarkable lifetime achievements.

When Jesus teaches about dying to be reborn, losing our lives in order to save them, he's flipping our assumptions. One successfully gains "life," we believe, by relentlessly pursing it, and surely not by losing it. In fact, "losing it" has become an idiom for a momentary loss of composure and control, resulting in anger, disorientation, or a disruption in predictable behavior. It can damage pathways for succeeding or gaining one's life and a negative factor if shared by another person providing a reference for a job application.

Other versions of losing it are reactions to modern culture's fixation on predictable orderliness in the world of commerce as well as in organized religion. In 2018, Australian music producer Paul Nicholas Fisher (just "Fisher" is his performing title) released the song "Losing It." It shot to the top of charts in Australia, moved around the world, was nominated for the Grammy's Best Dance Song in 2019, and was in the top twenty-five US dance/electronic songs. I joined over eighteen million others in viewing this on YouTube. It's a throbbing, electronic piece running four minutes and eight seconds that's made for dance clubs. The lyrics are about as profound as some Christian praise songs: "I'm losing it" is repeated eight times. That's all.

I've read that it was nearly impossible to go to a music festival or dance club without hearing this song. But I can imagine, before the onset of the coronavirus pandemic, the scene of hundreds crowded together in dancing ecstasy repeating the lyrics, "I'm losing it." Clearly, there are different ways of losing it, and not all find life.

Pilgrimage, however, imparts fresh meaning and practice into these ancient words of wisdom. Walking a pilgrim's path in life surrenders what is, more accurately, the myth of control. Our desire for control becomes the problem rather than the solution. Arranging our life in carefully controlled segments with predictable outcomes or destinations rarely works as planned in any event. As David Whyte writes in his poem "What to Remember When Waking," "What you can plan is too small for you to live." After all, who plans to fall in love? How many vocational paths are shaped by chance, unpredictable encounters at pivotal moments? Freeing ourselves from the desire to know, regulate, and shape the future opens one's journey to unexpected, grace-filled discoveries. Life is saved because you lose it.

"For me," writes Sister Simone Campbell, "the contemplative perspective leads to letting go of my desires and control while opening to the gift of the moment. My consistent learning is that behind the loss is always a surprise, opening into something new." Sister Simone is the executive director of Network, a group founded by Roman Catholic nuns and members of religious orders who established a presence in Washington, DC, witnessing to the claims of God's justice and peace. They've also become known nationally through their "Nuns on the Bus" tours raising awareness of issues of justice and public policy throughout the country. Sister Simone nurtures a grounded spirituality that's reflected in her work. Where loss can also be surprise.

The pilgrim's loss of control is a liberating form of surrender. It is born from the countercultural conviction that we are not the masters of our own destiny. Rather, in relinquishing ourselves to the messiness of lived experience, and to circumstances we know we are unable to control, we discover a Presence that has already enfolded us, sustained us, and gone ahead of us. It's grace. Pilgrims through the ages have grasped this or been grasped by it. Describing those Celtic wanderers for the love of God, Christine Valters Paintner puts it this way:

> *The wandering saints set forth without destination—often getting into small boats with no oars or rudder, called coracles—and trusted themselves to "the currents of divine love." They surrendered themselves completely to elements of wind and ocean . . . In this profound practice, God becomes both destination and way, companion and guiding force.*

I learned a definition of grace in seminary: God's "unmerited favor" toward people. God takes the initiative toward us in spite of ourselves, and that's called grace. This overturned imbedded practices in the church that tried to earn or, with indulgences, even buy God's favor.

The truth of this disruptive and liberating impulse, however, gets wrapped up in theological debate. For Protestants, the verse "by grace are you saved through faith" was a constantly quoted proof text to explain why Catholics were wrong. In the process, grace became weaponized as a theological canon instead of functioning as a way of life. The irony is that many of those most ardent in their defense of the doctrine of grace have been the least graceful in their stance toward others not seen as part of their tradition.

However, the theological differences between Protestants and Catholics over the doctrine of grace, for centuries so contentious, have been largely overcome. In 1999, the Lutheran World Federation and the Vatican's Pontifical Council for Promoting Christian Unity made church history by signing a joint declaration stating that the Lutheran and Catholic churches had come to share "a common understanding of our justification by God's grace through faith in Christ." In a movement of the Spirit, centuries-old mutual condemnations and theological stereotypes about each other were now formally ended in this official agreement, at least between those Lutheran churches and the Vatican's authorities. The proclamation, now, is that we are saved by grace through faith.

I traveled to the town of Wittenberg, where Luther nailed the famous Ninety-Five Theses to the door of the Castle Church on October 31, 1517, along with other delegates to the General Council of the World Communion of Reformed Churches. This global body represents 233 denominations and about one hundred million people from the world's Reformed and Presbyterian churches, another major stream emerging from the Reformation.

Gathering in the crowded Stadtkirche, several hundred delegates from around the world heard Rev. Najla Kassab, a female pastor from Lebanon, preach from the pulpit used by Martin Luther. Then we witnessed the leadership of the WCRC and of the Vatican officially sign the document affirming that these Reformed and Presbyterian churches were joining with the Joint Declaration on Justification.

Grace unfolds, loosens. Grace—God's unmerited favor—has no preconditions. Grace is dangerous and threatening to those desiring clear, binary systems of theological predictability.

A pilgrimage liberates grace from the confines of doctrine and embodies this foundational reality of God in lived experience. And grace liberates the pilgrim. The one who walks discovers how to receive grace, usually in unexpected ways that one cannot control. Grace comes when the pilgrim receives "favor," meaning something that sustains, blesses, and enlivens one in the midst of the daily journey, that comes not because they worked for it, earned it, or deserved it, but rather as a free gift. When you lose life, you find it through unpredictable grace.

On a pilgrimage, and in all of life, hospitality is the expression of embodied grace. On the Camino I tasted what that was like. On our first day leaving Ponderrada, our quartet followed the way through local farmlands. A woman tending a long row of ripe tomatoes greeted us, and we tried in our broken Spanish to respond. Then she suddenly cut four large ripe tomatoes from the vine and gave them to us, saying "Buen camino." We sliced and ate this delicious fruit of the vine at special times over the next three days.

On the second day we headed through Vega de Valcarce before a hard climb up a mountain. Outside the church young girls in matching T-shirts had a mission of squeezing fresh orange juice from ripe oranges, giving the refreshing drink to each pilgrim coming by. I offered to pay, like a guilty sinner, and was dismissed with a graceful laugh.

Alone on the third day on a difficult mountain pathway shrouded in a fog, entering the region of Gilicia, I went into a café, exhausted. After I ordered a café con leche, some orange juice, and a local pastry, two men from Spain on the Camino sat at a nearby table and we struck up a conversation. My poor Spanish was equal to their English, resulting in fragmented conversation about US politics, augmented with smiles and laughter. They moved on, continuing their pilgrimage. After another ten minutes or so, I was ready to leave and asked the waitress for my check. She shook her head no. The two Spanish sojourners had paid for me.

Such simple acts punctuated each day, creating vivid memories. Nothing spectacular, but so moving, and always unexpected and unpredictable. These responses came from strangers, who owed me nothing. I couldn't earn or pay for what I was receiving. I was given lessons in grace.

There's a formative biblical story about hospitality in the book of Genesis, when Abraham and Sarah, following their own journey, were making their home on the plain in Mamre. Three strangers came by, and Abraham insisted on offering them hospitality, providing water, cakes baked by Sarah, milk, and then a calf to share. The strangers turned out to be messengers from God, and some theologians have seen in these guests the presence of the Trinity. Soon the table of hospitality was turned, as Abraham and Sarah were given a gift: a promise by God that Sarah, in her old age, would bear a son.

In the familiar story, hospitality is both the presence of embodied grace and the avenue for discovering God's presence and promise. The theme of showing hospitality, love, and justice to strangers in the land echoes throughout the stories and teachings of the Hebrew Bible. God's grace— that is, God's favor toward humanity—is intended to be embodied in how God's people treat those who are strangers, sojourners, migrants, pilgrims.

What grace means, at its core, is that we can't save ourselves. Theology can encapsulate grace within doctrinal debates and easily empty it of meaning and effect in our daily lives. As pilgrims, however, we walk into the lived experience of being sustained by undeserved favor from strangers. In that, we don't just learn about God's grace; we taste its reality—even in ripe tomatoes, fresh orange juice, and free café con leche.

The lessons of being sustained by unpredictable grace on unfamiliar pathways calling for the relinquishment of control extend far beyond an individual's pilgrim journey. And not only pilgrims but churches and faith-based organizations can gain rich insight into how they function and might grow by understanding their institutional life as one of being on a pilgrimage. And that's counter to prevailing views of how to manage and strategically govern these bodies.

Prior to the coronavirus pandemic, I spoke at a gathering of a large progressive denomination. Before I did, I wanted to have a sense of what some of the leaders were reading. Among the books they mentioned was *Canoeing the Mountains: Christian Leadership in Uncharted Territory* by Tod Bolsinger.

The book describes how the future facing US faith communities will look nothing like the past, and how their journey will travel into uncharted territory. As churches have faced the eruption of the coronavirus pandemic, this journey into an unknown landscape has become the reality in ways never foreseen. Bolsinger uses the Lewis and Clark expedition as a guiding metaphor: they assumed the unexplored territory they were entering would be similar to the familiar land they were leaving. But those expectations were shattered by landscapes they could not imagine. The expedition's success came from their ability to adapt to the unexpected, learn from loss, let go of past assumptions, and persistently press ahead. It meant canoeing the mountains.

For those intrepid faith leaders who consider their work as the work of pilgrimage, that task is similar. The journey ahead will be nothing like what it has been in the familiar territory of the past. It requires "going off the map," where adaptation is everything, and leaders must develop the inner qualities of both conviction and calm to stay on course and inspire trust. They learn and are transformed in the process in a relational style of leadership. For Bolsinger, this is how the church can journey out of its past comfortable captivity to Christendom and discover a future of courageous missional engagement in the rapidly changing culture.

I could see why this particular group of faith leaders was drawn to a book like *Canoeing the Mountains*. It fits my understanding of how to imagine the journey toward the future of any resonant Christian presence in our culture. But for me, it makes even more sense to frame this journey as a pilgrimage.

Beyond religious institutions' immersion into styles and tools of modern organizational planning, control, and results that are measured. Beyond a rationale for determining how to allocate resources. Beyond a strategic plan that can guide to a future five or ten years ahead. Beyond job descriptions for staff resulting in disciplined work with clear objectives. In short, beyond predictability and control is something like pilgrimage, something like grace.

As general secretary of the Reformed Church in America, I began my service looking for clear direction, singular mission, and guiding vision. A collaborative effort resulted, as I was part of drafting a compelling mission and vision statement eventually leading to a ten-year goal we described as Our Call. This focused resources, energy, and staff around congregational revitalization, new church development, and building a multicultural future. We reimagined leadership development. In a denomination burdened with an organizational culture equipped well for the past, some promising and fruitful change resulted.

Today, I'm far less convinced of the wisdom and efficacy of these methods. It's naïve and even audacious, I now think, to adopt a ten-year or a five-year goal and think that this is possible. Change comes far too fast and is inherently unpredictable. I have little faith that churches know how to measure outcomes, and less confidence that they have the wisdom to know which outcomes to measure. Now, I would put more energy into helping faith communities develop the spiritual depth and the practices of discernment necessary in order to adapt to the challenges of the future, and far less energy into strategic planning.

At a daylong retreat, I had a conversation with one of the more gifted pastors I know. Her congregation, once comfortably dormant, now is thriving with ministry, outreach, engagement with the community, and growth, and her leadership has been the catalyst. But she said to me, "I no longer have a plan. I'm not even sure a lot of the time what we're doing. But I just keep discovering what's before us and try to take the next step."

Religious organizations attuned to God's preferred and promised future will find themselves on a pilgrimage. Normalcy and routine are left behind. Faithful patience is required, one step at a time, resisting superficial formulas for instant transformation. Past systems of security, needed at an earlier stage, now can be relinquished. Attention becomes rooted in concrete practices rather than abstract theological debates. Enough space is opened in organizational life for the Spirit to shatter safe expectations. Slowly, faith communities learn to trust that unpredictable grace will sustain their organizational pilgrimage on pathways in uncharted territory toward a new land.

More saturated with God's grace, and less subject to our manipulation and control, pilgrimage is like a lens for affording a different view of reality. The concrete practice of pilgrimage is like a school for developing the tools, sensitivities, and intuitions necessary for embracing a world that, at its core, is sustained by this grace, embodied in concrete, unpredictable ways. On pilgrim pathways, we learn the myth of control, the wisdom of relinquishment, the promise of the unpredictable, and the embodiment of grace.

Chapter 8

A Reenchanted World

This water is holy. Entering the room where pilgrims can be immersed fully in water flowing from the spring of the grotto, kind and graceful men greeted me. My poor French was comparable to their halting English, but they conveyed the spirit of this place, which transcends language. I disrobed. Covered with a towel, I placed my feet on the second step of a rectangular pool, somewhat larger than a coffin and filled with cold water. Crossing myself I said, "In the name of the Father, the Son, and the Holy Spirit," and offered a silent prayer, as is the practice. The attendants held my hands as I stepped to the end, sat, and immersed myself.

They pulled me out of the water as I stood and then offered me more holy water to drink. It was cool, pure, and as good as the water from Iceland or Norway that costs $2.09 a bottle. Then, following form, they said the Hail Mary with me, as I mumbled the words to hide my uncertainty about all the phrases. But I did know how to pray out loud the standard prayer, "Saint Bernadette, pray for me," before stepping out of the water. In the dressing room, three young men from Italy were waiting their turn, and a younger man from France, moving with a constraining limp.

Walking outside, looking at the fast-flowing river swollen by December rain, and the massive cathedral on its banks, built directly above the shallow stone cave called a grotto, I felt an overwhelming sense of peace and contentment. All was well, and all everywhere would be well. This was what writers like Richard Rohr call a nondualistic moment. Others long before have used similar language describing this oneness. Julian of Norwich's words, "all manner of things shall be well," resonated.

Sometimes walking. Sometimes water. Sometimes dirt. The life of the pilgrim is a life lived in the elements. Still in the contentment of the moment I walked across the Gave de Pau River on a bridge that had wire mesh sides, like the fence enclosing the concrete play area at my grade school. But woven into the mesh were various ribbons, locks, strings of beads, and other mementos left by passing pilgrims. It was a familiar sight. I had seen similar ones on the way to Santiago, and at Chimayó, New Mexico.

A "chapel of candles" was on the other bank, consisting of small pavilions, with plexiglass sides to protect from wind, holding rows of burning candles. And these were not votives, but candles running from about fifteen to thirty inches tall, costing "donations" of three to six euros. While typically not a religious candle lighter, except for those little white ones with paper bibs during "Silent Night" on Christmas Eve, I put in donations for tall ones for my wife and kids and watched them burn. It's said that such a candle is a way of continuing one's prayer.

Growing up in Lourdes, France, Bernadette Soubirous was a fourteen-year-old illiterate girl when the spiritual visions began. Her family was nearly destitute, housed in a former prison. On February 11, 1858, she went to a grotto in a rocky hillside near the river while gathering firewood and had a vision of a young woman appearing to her. These "apparitions" continued eighteen times in the next several weeks, with simple messages. Slowly, Bernadette, her priest, and eventually a skeptical church became convinced that Bernadette was seeing the Virgin Mary.

On February 25, 1858, Bernadette experienced the ninth apparition. She was told to go to the back of the grotto, dig in the earth, and drink the water. The muddy water gradually became clear, breaking forth into a flowing spring. Three days later, Catherine Latapie, a woman from nearby Loubajac, was prompted to go to the grotto with Bernadette. Meeting her at dawn, Catherine knelt and prayed at the grotto. Her right arm and fingers had been paralyzed. When she went to wash her hands in the spring, she suddenly regained feeling, and her paralysis was healed. The spring water has flowed ever since, the same water that flowed over me.

Today more pilgrims flock to Lourdes than any other Christian site, except for Rome. Between four and six million come each year. The town has only seventeen thousand inhabitants, but more hotels than any other city in France except Paris. Up to one hundred thousand volunteers are present during the spring and summer, and among the pilgrims are about eighty thousand who struggle with debilitating illnesses or some kind of physical infirmity. Special housing is provided for them, and they are brought in wheelchairs and stretchers to Masses and the large processions, including a nightly torch light procession of thousands in the height of the pilgrim season. In one year, 350,000 pilgrims experience the water immersion, like I did in December when few pilgrims were present. Pilgrims drink the water, and most fill bottles and jugs, readily available at countless souvenir shops, to take home. Lourdes confers holiness on water.

Ever since the visit of Catherine Latapie, healings have taken place in Lourdes. As a Protestant steeped in the Reformed tradition and molded by the worldview of modernity, I was wired to be skeptical of healings, whether in Lourdes or at Pentecostal revivals. That skepticism is matched, however, by the official Catholic Church. One hundred and twenty years ago, a Medical Investigations Office was established at Lourdes and still functions. It examines every notification of a cure brought to them to see if it is actually miraculous, according to their strict criteria. Possible cases are then passed on to the International Medical Commission for further review. Over seven thousand potential cases of miraculous cures have been brought to this process. Only seventy have been officially declared by the Catholic Church as miracles, where no other explanation is deemed possible.

Countless other pilgrims coming to Lourdes experience healing in a variety of ways, in body, mind, and spirit, without being documented. For instance, Ryan Kuja, a graduate of the Seattle School of Theology and Psychology, shared with me online his account of having a serious blood clotting disorder. He traveled to Lourdes, prayed at the grotto, and heard a voice telling him to worry no longer. Upon returning home and doing testing with his hematologist, no trace of the former condition was found. Later he went on the Camino de Santiago with an interreligious group of pilgrims and wrote about the experience in an article, "A Pilgrim's Blood and Eschatological Hope."

Healings that seem miraculous are like icons. They open our minds and our hearts to a penetrating, illuminating understanding of reality. Our material and spiritual worlds, kept so efficiently separated by the worldview of modernity, intersect one another as an integrated whole. Catching glimpses of this in water deemed to be holy, we then wonder whether we are touching upon what is ultimately real and true. The material stuff of this world, objectified as inert and lifeless, becomes reenchanted, even in the water we drink, which once was made into wine.

Pilgrims thirst for this. A pilgrimage is defined as going to a place that is expected to be holy. Such holiness is never ethereal, but present in tangible ways, in bones that still live, in dirt that carries life, in water that confers healing. The pilgrim encounters these in the presence of others before and after in a timeless procession. Healing, renewal, and transformation, integrating body, mind, and spirit in embodied ways, then results as other physical practices are engaged: candles lit, knees bent on stone, prayers like smoke, going up.

Where in one place water is holy, in another it may be dirt. Such is the ground of El Santuario de Chimayó, a church and shrine tucked away in a valley in northern New Mexico. Walking into the small sanctuary, only sixty feet long and twenty-four feet wide, feels like walking back two centuries. Stepping through a wooden doorway where hundreds of thousands have passed, the poorly lit interior with a wooden beamed ceiling has walls lined with paintings, wooden retablos, a glass coffin holding a statue of Jesus, and an ancient crucifix, Nuestro Señor de Esquipulas, forming the altarpiece. It's the opposite of the Moravian Church in Christiansfeld, Denmark.

My wife, daughter, and I make our way to the altar, adorned with art expressive of Mexican culture meshed with Spanish Catholicism. We turn left, walking through a door out of the sanctuary into an adjoining room. There, a narrow doorway to the right leads to another small room. In the center, a circular pit the circumference of a large milk pail is filled with brown dirt. We bend down and kneel. My daughter fills a small glass container with the dirt and takes it back to her home in Grand Rapids, Michigan.

The rectangular space outside the room holding the holy dirt has scores of crutches hanging from its walls, along with pictures and testimonials of those who have been on pilgrimage to Chimayó and found healing. Daily, pilgrims as well as curious tourists come to this small church. They pray, go into the side room and fill small jars, plastic sandwich bags, empty prescription pill bottles, or Tupperware containers with dirt. Legend has it that the dirt miraculously keeps refilling. In truth, volunteers from the church go to nearby hills to dig dirt and regularly replenish the small pit in the side chapel. In a year, twenty-five to thirty tons of dirt are taken away by pilgrims from El Santuario de Chimayó and held holy.

According to tradition, in 1810 a Franciscan friar, Bernardo Abeyta, saw a strong light shining from a hillside. Going there, he dug and uncovered a large crucifix with a brown-skinned Jesus, which came to be known as Nuestro Señor de Esquipulas. The Santuario was built there with a space for the dirt, considered holy, holding a healing presence as miraculous cures were experienced.

Later discoveries found that a priest from Esquipulas, in Guatemala, was an early missionary in the Chimayó valley, preaching and carrying a large crucifix. But he was killed by local Indians. In 1810 the Santa Cruz River flooded, likely unearthing the body of the priest and the crucifix.

In World War II, many young men from northern New Mexico who were conscripted into the army fought in the

Philippines. With its fall to the Japanese, thousands were captured. Hundreds from New Mexico died on the Bataan Death March, and more languished in prison camps. The church in Chimayó had been dedicated to El Santo Niño de Atocha. This comes from the story of a young boy who dressed like a pilgrim and was thought to be the young Jesus, miraculously delivering food to needy prisoners. His image hangs in the Santuario de Chimayó. So, throughout the state of New Mexico, mothers, fathers, and relatives of those missing prayed to Santo Niño and promised to make a pilgrimage to Chimayó if their loved ones returned. Likewise, in the prison camps, the young men familiar with Chimayó offered similar prayers, promising to make pilgrimages there. And many, both in the camps and back home, reported seeing visions of imprisoned loved ones held in the light, like the light that shone over the hills in 1810. In the aftermath of the war, pilgrimages to El Santuario de Chimayó accelerated.

A statue of a pilgrim, reminiscent of those on the Camino de Santiago, stands outside the sanctuary, not far from the area for accessible parking. Below the figure on a plaque is this quote:

> Come pilgrims from the four corners of the earth. The Lord has invited us to walk to the shrine of love in Chimayó. Here we will find the "holy dirt" that strengthens us and purifies the faith that takes away our pain.

Each year three hundred thousand people visit Chimayó, making it the most important Catholic pilgrimage site in the US. During Holy Week tens of thousands of pilgrims from throughout New Mexico and beyond make their way to the Santuario. A few carry wooden crosses over their shoulders. Many are devout Catholics. Others rarely attend church. Some Protestant churches in the region, like the one I attend in Santa Fe, send groups on short pilgrimages. Nearly all make the pilgrimage by walking, because they consider El Santuario de Chimayó to be a holy destination.

Every year since she was a child, Diane Cordova has made this pilgrimage. "This place is powerful. A lot of things have happened here, so that's what keeps us coming," she said. "I know one day I'm going to have a miracle in that place. I probably already have and just don't know it."

In his traditional Native American dress, Victor Guzman comes to the site and explains his motivation and prayer: "The way things are right now . . . the world is drifting away from God bit by bit."

David Griego has made the pilgrimage to Chimayó for over fifteen years. But more recently, he's dedicated this holy walk and prayer to his wife, Joyce, who was diagnosed with stage two multiple sclerosis.

In the spring of 2020, word that the annual Holy Week pilgrimage to Chimayó was canceled due to the coronavirus pandemic came as a devastating loss to thousands of pilgrims.

Over the years the grounds around the church have been expanded to welcome the growing number of pilgrims to Chimayó. An outdoor worship area accommodates many for Catholic Mass, a shrine is devoted to Vietnamese pilgrims from the region, and places for photos and memories of those held in prayer are provided.

But El Santuario de Chimayó is best known for its dirt. Even before Bernardo Abeyta unearthed the crucifix, Native Americans had long honored the land in this location as sacred, with healing power. The dirt now sanctified for Christians by the crucifix it held continues as a tangible, material sign imbued with a holy, healing presence.

The dirt in Chimayó reminded me of the ground at Mount Tabieorar in Nigeria. There the founder of the church, Josiah Ositelu, received a vision in 1925. The space was set apart, considered holy ground. Other than the annual Tabieorar Festival, it's not used; no shrines or churches fill the space. But when one hundred thousand pilgrims gather there, their shoeless feet can feel the ground that carries sacred significance.

One of the things that devout pilgrims to Santiago de Compostela believe is that the bones of Saint James are living. They were discovered in about 813, when a hermit of Galicia, now part of northern Spain, saw stars seemingly dancing over a field, over a marble ark. An investigation ensued. Eventually the local bishop determined the decapitated remains held in the coffin to be that of the apostle James. For Christian Europe during medieval times, this was one of the most significant religious events.

How those bones ended up in northern Spain is a story, or legend, filled with marvel and imagination. Narratives about what happened to the apostles after Pentecost pick up where the New Testament stops. Thomas went to India. Mark went to Egypt. And James went to Spain. There may be faint historical collaboration for the legends, but when I've talked to Christians in India, Egypt, and Spain, doubts are regarded as heresy.

James's sojourn in Spain is made more historically problematic by a bothersome verse in the book of Acts, which recounts that Herod had James beheaded. The legend, however, recounts how James did indeed preach throughout Spain, but returned to Judea in time to meet his appointment with Herod's sword in about 44 CE. Then his followers took his head and the rest of his body and carried them to a boat. Here again, the oars were missing, as were the rudder and a steersman. The boat set out and remarkably found its way across the Mediterranean, through Gibraltar, and all the way up to the coast of today's northern Spain, where it landed. Followers, legend has it, found it and placed the decapitated body away, where it remained for the next eight hundred years.

The Prado Museum in Madrid is one of the world's famous repositories of art. In a section of medieval art in Room 051A is a powerful piece, *The Embarkation of the Body of Saint James the Greater at Jaffa*. The painting shows James's followers taking his severed head and body and placing them into a small boat with oarlocks but no oars. The work was painted by Martin Bernat in about 1480. Whatever its origins, this story was recounted and shared in art, the primary way narratives came alive for most people in both ancient and medieval Christian worlds.

As word of the discovery of James's bones spread through Europe, it had an electrifying effect. Pilgrims coming to the site experienced healings. Soon a church was constructed. Historians point to numerous economic and political reasons why this pilgrimage destination grew in popularity, especially drawing those who came from France, crossing the Pyrenees. By the tenth and eleventh centuries, five hundred thousand pilgrims were coming to Santiago de Compostela each year.

Such determined and costly devotion can only be understood through grasping the worldview of that time. Popular religious belief held that certain places were particularly holy, what we might call "thin spaces." The distance between heaven and earth, or, in modern thinking, the spiritual and the material, was joined through specific, tangible bridges. Often, these revolved around saints and apostles, including where they lived, where they were martyred, and where they were buried.

The bones of such persons were regarded as relics. These carried the living presence of the dead. In today's new-age parlance, we'd say they held a lot of spiritual energy. Being with such bones, in physical proximity, connected the pilgrim to not only to the saint, but, more importantly, to the saint's intercessionary access to God. So pilgrims walked to such places, even for hundreds and hundreds of miles.

The historicity of the story of St. James's bones can be easily dismissed. And the belief that access to God's presence was more certain at relics of a saint in a distant site than at one's local church or home was forcefully rejected by the Reformation. Further, the crass commercialization of "relics" numbering in the tens of thousands—straw from the Bethlehem manger, a twig from the burning bush, a splinter from the "true" cross, milk from the Virgin Mary—often rendered the sacred profane.

Yet the stories of Santiago de Compostela, Chimayó, Lourdes, Mount Tabieorar, and countless other places reveal the hunger today for faith that has embodied expressions. In modern societies that have become disenchanted and numb to any spiritual presence, these are seen as those bridges to the sacred. Beyond the sacred water or sacred relics, the experience of being *on* a pilgrimage, and not just in reaching the final destination, opens the traveler to the pervasive sacramental nature of life as one by one, the restrictive inhibitions of modernity are left behind.

People today yearn to taste and touch religious faith and not just hear about it. Secular modernity deconstructs theological belief systems and eliminates acceptable space for the holy. Reality is regarded as one-dimensional. But an instinctive longing for the sacred, for what Rudolf Otto called the "numinous," cannot be suppressed indefinitely. It leaches out, sometimes in strange and bizarre ways, part of an undercurrent of spiritual unease and thirst. Its satisfaction won't come rationally, or in slick, modern church buildings displaying the culture's version of success. Rather, it's seen in expressions and practices of an embodied faith that open sacramental space between heaven and earth.

At the grotto in Lourdes, where Bernadette had her apparitions of Mary, dark gray stone frames the sides and interior walls. Water drips slowly over parts. Pilgrims come, one by one, and as they walk from one side of the grotto to the other, their fingers trace the surface of the rock continually. I did not see a single pilgrim who did not touch the rock surface. Millions have done so, and the surface has become smooth. The need to touch seems unquenchable. These stones speak.

At the Cathedral de Santiago, I walked up a narrow staircase, in a procession to the statue of St. James, looking out from above the altar and over the grave said to hold his bones. I touched it, like all the others. Some wrapped their arms around him.

The advice given at El Santuario de Chimayó is that pilgrims should not eat the holy dirt. Some do anyway. Most take it to their homes and then, perhaps with some water, spread it over a wounded knee, or on an inflamed stomach, or over a malignant breast.

I carried water home from Lourdes in a small plastic container with the blue insignia of the shrine on its side. It rested for two days on the shelf above my desk. Then, at an open house, a friend came by. Her brother, now living with her, was in critical shape with his systems seeming to be shutting down. She was taking every initiative she knew, medically and spiritually, to nurture his healing. I showed her the water, fresh from my visit to Lourdes and asked if I might share some. Her eyes filled with tears, and she left with a tiny glass jar, like those that hold single servings of jam, filled with the water.

I can't pretend to say anything, with any certainty, about the effects of water, or dirt, or tracing stone at a grotto, or putting an arm around a statue over an apostle's grave, or taking shoes off on holy ground. But I know this. These experiences, and so many more opened up on pilgrimages, explode the myth of a world rationally comprehensible, comprising inert matter and mobilized molecules in diverse forms. I'm willing to wonder about the myths undergirding pilgrim stories and practices.

It's the myths of modernity and rationality that need to be destroyed.

The experiences of a reenchanted world encountered on pilgrimages offer a portal to a far more pervasive truth. These are not just aberrations. Rather, they are clues to how the world really is. The interconnections of life, down to the quantum entanglement of particles mysteriously communicating information, to the synchronicity of trees in a forest somehow sharing warnings of danger to one another, to the scrutinized miracles at Lourdes defying any other explanation, point to a world where "material" and "spiritual" dimensions are always interconnected in a single, indivisible whole.

We can call this a sacramental view of reality. Christian tradition offers an edge in understanding this. At the center of our faith, material reality is imbued with spiritual significance and power. Bread from the fields, and fruit of the vine, which human hands have made. Water in a baptismal font. Oil anointed on one's head. All this is rooted in the incarnation, where eternal word is united with human flesh. Then we wonder, if some water can be holy, maybe all is. If some dirt is holy, maybe all the earth is sacred. And maybe stones, and icebergs, can cry out.

Richard Rohr perhaps says this best:

The need for physical, embodied practices seems universal. Across Christian history, the "Sacraments," as Orthodox and Catholics call them, have always been with us. Before the age of literacy started to spread in Europe in the sixteenth century, things like pilgrimage, prayer beads, body prostrations, bows and genuflections, "blessing oneself" with the sign of the cross, statues, sprinkling things with holy water, theatrical plays and liturgies, incense and candles all allowed the soul to know itself through the outer world—which we are daring to call "Christ." These outer images serve as mirrors of the Absolute, which can often bypass the mind. Anything is a sacrament if is serves as a Shortcut to the Infinite, hidden in something that is very finite.

Chapter 9

Leaving the Empire Behind

The Judean wilderness is harsh, desolate, and nearly barren. It's not just arid, like the high desert where I live in New Mexico, but more extreme in its heat, rocky terrain, and lack of moisture. The Jordan, which hardly qualifies as a river by normal definitions, flows by the eastern edge of the Judean wilderness and into the Dead Sea, which lies 1,400 feet below sea level and is filled with ten times more salt than the ocean. The Essenes, a Jewish sect seeking purity, withdrew to this area for their hermetical life. We know of them today primarily because of the discovery of the Dead Sea Scrolls at Qumran. When I walked up toward the caves thought to be their ancient colony just northwest of the Dead Sea, the sun beat down on the rocky terrain with unremitting intensity.

It was in this wilderness landscape that John the Baptist retreated and proclaimed his radical message of repentance by the Jordan, baptizing those who responded. While the exact location isn't known, the area is about fifteen to twenty miles from Jerusalem. A day's walk. Many during his time made the trek, drawn by his denunciation of the corruption of the religious and political establishment in Jerusalem, and his call to be washed clean of hypocrisy and disobedience. He warned of harsh judgment and minced no words about the "vipers brood" making up the elites holding sway in the capital.

Why was this voice crying from the wilderness? In part, because in that extreme landscape, John was freer from the oppressive presence of the Empire and the watchful eyes of complicit religious rulers. John was certainly speaking the truth about power, but he wasn't yet speaking the truth directly to power. In the Judean wilderness he was a safe distance away, like others in Jewish history who had sought refuge there.

Those leaving Jerusalem to travel to the wilderness to hear John the Baptist were making a pilgrimage of sorts. They were walking to a living person they considered holy, in the place where he was issuing his call to repentance. These pilgrims came wondering what they would hear and expecting the possibility of their God's special presence through this prophet in this remote place.

As they walked, they were leaving the Empire behind. Like John, they were freeing themselves, at least for a few days, from the intrusive, oppressive power of Roman occupation and the complicity of those religious leaders trying to curry enough favor with Roman authorities to preserve their own religious power and all the material wealth that came with it.

Sure, Rome also occupied the Judean wilderness, and it was relatively close to Jerusalem. But Rome had little interest or presence in this barren, forsaken land.

The detachment that accompanies a pilgrimage can give a person clarity about the social and political life they have left behind, even temporarily. Perhaps John was in the wilderness not only because he had greater freedom of righteous speech there, but also because it required people to physically remove themselves from the routines of life in Jerusalem that had become callous to God's righteousness and head to another place. Once out by the Jordan River, they could see their religious and political life for what it really was—a compromised system that had become morally bankrupt and spiritually impotent. Their need for repentance was understood more clearly from the banks of the Jordan than from within the walls of the city of David, with its garrisons of Roman centurions.

After a season John returned to Jerusalem, where his truth and witness were heard more directly by those he was condemning. His direct accusations on the lack of moral values in government leadership landed him in prison, and eventually he was beheaded. But John's practice had reversed the direction of seeking the holy.

For centuries the people of Israel made pilgrimages to Jerusalem and its temple, particularly for festivals and holy days. But John called people away from Jerusalem, to the Judean wilderness, to discover God's holy presence there through immersion in water and the distance of place. Those whose lives were transformed left behind the compromised and complicit ways of living that were leading to death.

The movement of some pilgrims away from the power of the Empire and into the wilderness was also present in the early church. Monks and hermits turned their backs on the comforts of settled life and walked instead to the desert seeking lives of simplicity and prayer, freed from lure of material wealth and ease. Their inspiring examples resulted in one of the earliest forms of Christian pilgrimage as curious believers set out on journeys to visit these holy mentors and absorb some of their spiritual wisdom.

One of these desert fathers, St. Antony of Egypt, was considered an early founder of the monastic movement. As a young man, he withdrew from society, eventually living for twenty years near the Nile on a deserted mountain. But his reputation for holiness began to grow, drawing pilgrims to him, some of whom began to live in nearby caves or cells. Reluctantly, Antony organized them into a community as a precursor to monastic life. Such pilgrims were moving away from the reach of imperial reign in search of spiritual holiness shaped by physical detachment.

Some of these examples were even more extreme and bizarre. St. Simeon Stylites from Syria, living in the early fifth century, left a monastery for even more austere conditions in a hut, where it is said he didn't eat or drink and stood upright throughout Lent. Pilgrims flocked to him, but he tried to avoid them, changing locations. Eventually he climbed up and lived on top of pillars. This only increased the desire of pilgrims to see him, and finally he held daily audiences from atop his perch, some fifty feet high. This commitment to extreme physical detachment from society in the quest for holiness became a compelling attraction for early Christian pilgrims.

The conversion of Constantine in 312, of course, began to attract Christians to the power of the Empire where Christianity was embraced and soon requisite for religion, law, and government, resulting in compromising the teachings of Jesus and seducing those of the church into baptizing the power of the state and its rulers. This is a legacy we still struggle with today. Yet the pilgrimage away from the power of the Empire, reflected in John the Baptist's movement to the Judean wilderness, continued centuries later with certain streams of believers.

Even as Helena, Constantine's mother, made claims of recovering Jesus's tomb as well as his cross, and making Jerusalem a center of Christian veneration, some monks and hermits were recentering the quest for holiness elsewhere, through their withdrawal to the desert. Growing numbers of pilgrims attracted to the desert left behind the trappings of the Empire, whether intentionally or not, even after it had been "Christianized."

For those on pilgrimage today, we also face the choice of whether our path will leave the Empire behind. Here I don't mean only a physical pilgrimage to a destination like Santiago de Compostela, Chimayó, or elsewhere, although those do involve walking away from the securities of our normal lives. Rather, in the pilgrimage of our life's journey, we all find ourselves, to varying degrees, enmeshed in the grasp of what rightly can be called an Empire—an Empire that threatens our own fullness as well as the earth's life-sustaining capacities.

The language of "Empire" can seem incendiary to pragmatic ears, to those who take note of global economic progress alleviating poverty in historic ways, to those who trust in ongoing technological solutions to our most threatening challenges. But that is only to look at a subset of a larger understanding. The modern global economy does function like an Empire. It contains the story of colonialization, of land rule, of slavery, of the genocidal destruction of marginalized and indigenous peoples. It contains the story of the creation of more wealth for the wealthy, even while poverty levels, prior to the coronavirus epidemic, were slowly declining.

Some stark statistics tell the story. The world's wealthiest persons, with over $100,000 in assets, comprise 10 percent of the world's population but own 84 percent of the world's wealth. Those with less than $10,000 of wealth make up 64 percent of the world's population but own only 2 percent of the global wealth. Further, income of the richest 1 percent of the world has grown twice as fast as the bottom 50 percent; income inequality continues to rise. This is how Empires function.

Empires formerly were associated with nation-states such as the British Empire. But no longer. Today there's a web of global economic power, linking together the affluent managers of commerce in Western societies as well as places like Japan, South Korea, and Taiwan with the fast-growing economies of China, India, and elsewhere. The interdependence of these economies is indissoluble. Just ask any owner of a medium or large business in the US how many components and parts of its supply chain are outsourced to China, or elsewhere.

This global network of economic relationships is undergirded by a common culture. Its articles of faith are endless material consumption and everlasting economic growth. Those shape the religious creed of the global economy. A one-dimensional lifestyle riveted on the material fulfillment of human needs and reflected in ubiquitous malls and McDonald's transcending national, cultural, and geographic boundaries is the promise of this Empire.

But the secular faith of this culture in limitless consumption and unstoppable growth is false. The continuing, mindless practice of this faith is leading to the destruction of the earth's carefully calibrated balance that sustains and undergirds life. We know this now, from volumes of scientific reports, decades of study by expert international bodies, and the undeniable evidence of receding glaciers, melting ice-caps, disappearing atolls and islands, intensifying forest fires, more extreme hurricanes, higher floodwaters, prolonged drought, and much more. There are limits to growth, and the Empire is transgressing against them, endangering us all.

We need spiritual, social, economic, and, at times, geographic detachment from the grasp of the Empire, which shapes the normalcy of our lives and goes largely unnoticed except for when we separate recyclables or look at mileage ratings when we buy a new car.

Pilgrimages can help—actual ones, walking to a holy place, for a holy purpose. Just like those walking down the rocky paths of Judean mountains to find John the Baptizer at the Jordan, a dramatic change in place can give us a liberating perspective, and even a sacred experience to embody our repentance. Plus, when we're walking, our footprints don't emit carbon.

My most difficult climb on the Camino was a hike up a mountain to O'Cebreiro. On that August evening when we stopped at the albergue in La Faba, one of the pilgrims staying there had a guitar, and a sing-along began. They used their smartphones to get lyrics. But when they broke into Leonard Cohen's "Hallelujah," it gave me chills. Cohen's plaintive, wondering spirituality fit well. These pilgrims had walked away from the Empire, whether in Germany, Spain, the United States, or Australia, at least for the days of their Camino. Connection and community were valued; fast-paced consumerism was left behind. Pilgrimages can create space for a fresh and refreshing cluster of values, shared among emergent mini communities.

But pilgrims also return home after reaching their destination, unlike monks or hermits who make the choice of a permanent withdrawal. In the Middle Ages, "a pilgrimage was a rough test of faith, the most unpredictable and independent thing a person could do in a short life," wrote Timothy Egan in *A Pilgrimage to Eternity*. Traveling months to a site typically holding the relics of a saint, they carried not only a few belongings in a sack, but expectations for physical healing, forgiveness, reconciliation, or other ways in which closeness to the saint's spiritual power would transform their lives. And then, if protected from mortal danger, they returned.

The real "rough test of faith" came not in their ability to persevere in making such an arduous journey, but in the changes it made, or didn't make, when they were back home. Was life lived differently, freer from constraints imposed by normalcy, and more able to reflect in deeds and relationships the spiritual transformation they had experienced? Would these returning pilgrims have a transforming effect in the churches, villages, or manors where they lived?

We know John the Baptist didn't remain in the Judean wilderness by the Jordan, but returned, fatefully, to Jerusalem. After John baptized Jesus, with the Spirit descending and heavenly words proclaiming him as God's Son, Jesus went into his own wilderness experience for forty days (it's worth noting this is about as long as it takes to moderately walk the Camino from St. Jean Pied de Port to Santiago de Compostela).

Amidst the heat, rocky terrain, and isolation, Jesus's identity was tested and his inner reliance on God's power to save and direct was grounded. Then Jesus began his ministry in Galilee. After three years, and with a community of disciples, he journeyed to Jerusalem, confronting its religious and political powers with acts of healing and a saving message that broke their self-serving boundaries of righteousness, welcoming and including all whom God loved.

As pilgrims today, we also return home. We, and our friends ask, what is different? The challenge is whether the experience at Lourdes, or Santiago de Compostela, or Mount Tabieorar, or El Santuario de Chimayó, or elsewhere has had a transforming effect in our daily life, enmeshed as it is with the Empire. Put simply, have they been transformed in order to be transforming? Has temporary distance created the clarity, commitment, and strength to leave the Empire behind in the place where that is most difficult—at home? Has the temporary distance allowed us to walk the longer journey of a life in faith, at home?

Returning home from Lourdes, I listened to a presentation at our church, the United Church of Santa Fe, by Larry Rasmussen. Larry was the Reinhold Niebuhr Professor of Christian Ethics at Union Seminary and the author of *Earth-Honoring Faith*, a compelling and comprehensive work rethinking religious environmental ethics. He introduced a carbon offset program for members of our church and told us that the average US citizen emits 16.6 tons of CO_2 emissions per year, and much is from automobile and air travel. Achieving an individual zero carbon footprint is virtually impossible. But the costs of our carbon emissions can be "offset" through supporting efforts combatting climate change, like planting trees and supporting renewal energy resources.

So, Larry and others did the calculations. Offsetting an individual's carbon cost while sitting on an airplane comes to $8.00 for a three-hour flight. Flying from Santa Fe to Europe would be about $32.00. For car travel, offsetting five thousand miles, on average, comes to $16.00. The program invites members to contribute those amounts through the church to organizations like New Mexico Interfaith Power and Light and Trees New Mexico. I fly a lot. United Airlines typically credited me with about one hundred thousand miles per year. That's a lot of carbon to offset, but a small step in leaving the Empire behind. It's a rough test of faith.

St. Nicholas Church in Leipzig, Germany, has an eight-hundred-year history, including when Johann Sebastian Bach served as choirmaster from 1723 to 1750. Listening to the Bach compositions played on the church organ there in the summer of 2017 brought his long legacy of music to life. But the service was being held to commemorate another period of St. Nicholas's history—its crucial role in the fall of the East German Communist regime.

Beginning in the 1980s, Monday evening prayer services started in this famous downtown Lutheran church. Though kept under surveillance by the omnipresent East German police, the Stasi, the church was one of the few places offering a protected haven for gathering, reflection, and discussion, as well as worship and prayer. The Monday evening prayer services opened a space for conversation about human rights, democratic aspirations, and a yearning for social and political change, along with studying the Sermon on the Mount and biblical themes of justice and social righteousness.

By 1989, these prayer meetings had begun to swell, filling the church, even as the disaffection of East Germans with their regime was yearning for expression. On October 9th of that year, thousands gathered at the church, overflowing its pews and narrow balconies. Following the prayer service, they processed, armed only with candles. Thousands more joined them in the city center, moving in procession, confronting reinforced lines of riot police. But marching by candlelight requires one hand to hold the candle, and the other to protect it against wind and keep it burning. No one could carry anything threatening violence.

The gathering and procession of between seventy thousand and one hundred thousand was the largest one of its kind in East German history. The riot police had no response for prayerful, nonviolent marchers armed only with candles. They gave way, allowing the procession to go forward. More candlelight processions ensued throughout the country, and the courage of people's public action increased. Just one month later, the Berlin Wall fell. Most agree that the prayer service and candlelight processions beginning at St. Nicholas Church were a pivotal step in events that led eventually to the fall of the East German regime.

A detached space had been provided by St. Nicholas Church for the inner spiritual preparation, clarity of vision, and commitment required for these East Germans willing to begin walking away, publicly, from their Empire.

While pilgrimages can be described as going to a holy place, they are also steps made with a holy purpose. Seventy thousand or more marchers walking courageously around the Leipzig ring road were modern pilgrims whose steps became a public and political witness. Guided only by candles on an uncertain way forward, they were leaving behind a corrupt, oppressive political and economic order.

National City Church on Thomas Circle in Washington, DC, shares a neoclassical architectural style with St. Nicholas Church in Leipzig, but not the same long history. On May 24, 2018, it was overflowing with a gathering spilling outside onto its massive steps and beyond. They had come to affirm the declaration "Reclaiming Jesus," a public witness against the resurgence of white nationalism, bigotry, public deceit, and autocratic political power characterizing the Trump administration. The declaration grounded its resistance in the words, teaching, and authority of Jesus.

Weeks earlier, on Ash Wednesday, a small group had gathered at the New York apartment of Rev. Michael Curry, presiding bishop of the Episcopal Church. With Jim Wallis as a primary facilitator, we reflected on the moral and political crisis facing the nation in an atmosphere of prayer. Out of this safe space, the next morning we decided that a public plea, addressing the spiritual roots of the dangerous mood and political movement in the nation fomented by schism and white nationalism that held a religious fervor, needed to be written. When drafted and released in video format, it struck a moral nerve.

When the service of prayer and inspiration at National City Church finished, the leaders and those gathered inside were joined by hundreds more. About three thousand moved in a candlelit procession that night with holy purpose to the White House. There, the declaration was repeated in this act of public witness. It was a step forward, trying to leave the reigning political Empire behind.

The pathways in the lives of today's pilgrims first lead away, to places of detachment and withdrawal, yielding a grounding clarity about the world's realities and spiritual empowerment for the way forward. Then, faithful pilgrims return, walking into the public square with a transforming presence and witness. In the end, pilgrims leave the Empire behind not by cloistering themselves away in isolated retreat, but by walking into its centers of power with a resilient witness that has been liberated from its grasp.

In 2013 the Assembly of the World Council of Churches was hosted in Busan, Korea. It's a gathering that takes place once every seven years, a unique and critical encounter of global Christianity. The Assembly invited its member churches to engage together in a "pilgrimage of justice and peace." For the WCC to be committed to justice and peace was nothing new. However, setting this in the framework of pilgrimage was intentional, novel, and challenging. Since pilgrimage had deep roots in Christian tradition and growing contemporary interest and practice, it carried an ecumenical reach fitting with the WCC's vocation.

A guide was created to assist churches who wished to respond to the Assembly's invitation. A portion of the guide included the meaning and practice of pilgrimage:

> *Sacred pilgrimage is a form of faith development that involves both spiritual discernment and action. As such, it is both a destination and a process. As pilgrims we set out towards our objective believing that we will gain insight through encounter, meditation, and prayer. Along the way, we chance upon God in surprising places and unlikely people. In those moments, we do not always recognize God. Yet if we can be open to unexpected encounters, it is through them that we will discover renewed purpose for our lives and new possibilities for justice and peace. At the end of a pilgrimage we find ourselves in a place where we feel spiritually enriched; a place where we can engage in actions that contribute to transformation of our communities; a place where we are acting as faithful Christians.*

In years following the Busan Assembly, the WCC tried to reframe much of its work as an ongoing pilgrimage for justice and peace. Whether it was delegations raising human rights issues with oppressive governments or consultations in Artic regions and the South Pacific addressing climate change, these efforts were organized as part of this wider pilgrimage. Further initiatives in local settings launched pilgrimages to address specific issues of violence and injustice. All these became avenues, in one way or another, of assisting those wanting to leave the Empire behind in their pilgrimage of faith.

Walking on pilgrimages shaped by a holy purpose, and addressing stark injustices, ecological threats, racism, and violence all sustained by contemporary imperial power, has become in recent years a frequent avenue of witness and action. Beyond talking and writing, people want to walk in ways that embody their convictions and reveal the realities they wish to confront. The immigration crisis on the US border with Mexico has witnessed numerous cross-border pilgrimages designed for this purpose.

One such dramatic pilgrimage in 2016, El Camino del Inmigrante, moved from the Tijuana/San Diego border 150 miles north to downtown Los Angeles, dramatically highlighting the need to address the injustices of the broken immigration system. Rev. Alexia Salvatierra, one of the key organizers, said, "In the Camino, we are seeing so many people who are being moved by the Spirit to join the cause of justice; I believe it is God's moment for change to occur."

The witness of pilgrimages can initiate changes in society. As the popularity of pilgrimages continues to grow in our time, the danger is that they will become a new way for people to seek privatized spiritual experience. But pilgrimages are acts of public witness, where our feet do the talking. We are not walking for ourselves. Rather, like those Celtic pilgrims without oars, our stepping into the boat is a surrender to the currents of God's love. That love beckons us to leave the Empire behind for the promise of a divine reign of justice, healing, and peace. Whatever our holy destination, our walking itself opens pathways toward a liberating future intended by the Creator.

Chapter 10

Leaving Life

Pilgrimages call us away from our settled past and beckon us to a future place infused with a spiritual presence. For many early Christians, this was the catacombs in Rome, and later churches holding relics and the bones of apostles and saints. The sites of visions and apparitions conferred holiness on water, dirt, and ground. Healings were and continue to be associated with all these sacred spaces. Pilgrims journey there in search of wholeness of life, and the nearer presence of God.

Life's final pilgrimage completes this journey. We take a last step away from life as we know it and cross a threshold in the hope of entering a sacred space full of God's presence. A pilgrimage as a long journey to a sacred destination is one that, ultimately, prepares us to die. Along with the things we leave behind—from material possessions to our investment in our egos—the lessons we gain as we step forward teach us the most valuable and lasting truths of our pilgrimage. In our deepening understanding of the pilgrimage as a journey of life, the last thing we learn to leave behind is our life.

Making this final step in our pilgrimage with grace depends on learning to die before we die. In successive steps, the pilgrim is nudged to give up some level of control. That starts with the predictability of our normal lives. Then the abandonment of our reliance on a curated, virtual self. We give up our need for immediate solutions and instant gratification. We let go of secure identities shaped by life's early needs. We relinquish trying to control our journey through "right" creeds and rational systems of belief. We dismiss predictable piety that serves spiritual comfort over spiritual growth. We admit the folly of planning for expected outcomes that omit grace. We give up a view of reality that robs the world of its enchanted wonder. We liberate our lives and the lives of others from the control of the modern Empire.

At each of these steps, we discover life—true life made richer, fuller, freer, and filled with the Spirit's presence. All these steps, however, require that we die to our self in these various ways. We can describe this as our old self, or, as we have said, our false self. Or we can describe this, like Jesus did, as the grain of wheat that must fall and die if it is to bear abundant fruit. Such dying to self always means giving up some level of the control that we crave.

At times, this loss of control may be imposed on us in crisis. We may be crushed and nearly destroyed by addictions. A terrible tragedy or wrenching death of a loved one may strike us down. A fulfilling career may be abruptly and involuntarily taken from us. An unimaginable event like the coronavirus pandemic may completely undo us. Such circumstances of life break in upon us and, in the Psalmist's words, throw our life into the pit. And we can't control any of it.

For others, a persistent inward journey breaks open the illusions of one's life. Narcissistic needs of the ego are revealed. Private levels of deceit are exposed. Unquenchable strivings of ambition are confessed. The betrayal of treasured relationships becomes undeniable. In so many ways, our false self controls life and resolutely clings to power.

In one of these ways or another, we come to a point where we feel powerless. Some recognize this as the first of the twelve steps in recovery programs. It's the critical point of insight in the therapeutic process. And it's the true beginning of an authentic spiritual journey. Often it is all three.

Dying to the illusion of control, and to the false self, with the suffering that this may entail, is what opens pathways toward life. In the end, this prepares us for the final step in our journey, facing our physical death. A pilgrim's progress shows the way.

Of all my pilgrimages, the trip to Lourdes was my most unexpected and unlikely one. It had been off my spiritual and geographic radar, for I thought Lourdes was a destination for traditional Catholics caught up in tempting legends of cures. Souvenir shops with rosaries and statues of Mary were about the most I could imagine.

But as happens so often with pilgrimages, there was something quietly beckoning me. An inner need to visit that wouldn't dissipate, which then with a set of unforeseen circumstances suddenly presented the opportunity. My response to go had not been planned. I arrived not knowing what to expect, but knowing this: I had to move forward. A video at the welcome center gave me some orientation, but I walked out wondering where to go and what to do, with no crowds or lines of waiting pilgrims to guide me.

Lourdes is comprised of two primary cathedrals, one built on top of the other like an ecclesial wedding cake. Both are directly over the grotto. I decided to walk up massive stairways to the top; getting there, my knees nearly gave out, and my body felt vulnerable and weak. But the next day, following an English eucharistic service I found my way to benches outside the enclosed rooms, like bath houses, where the opportunity for "water immersion" was offered. I wrote about what happened next in a previous chapter, but not what led me to that point.

By this time, I felt completely out of control. How I had ended up here, leaving home in Santa Fe with a nudge of immediacy and quickly made plans, not even seventy-two hours earlier, seemed inexplicable. This was a pilgrimage now entering uncharted waters and without oars. The only option that felt possible was to step forward.

When I was gently led into the rectangular pool of water and then submerged, it was with surrender and relinquishment. I didn't know exactly what would happen. My thoughts went to baptism and, appropriately, to death. I was letting go.

Suddenly I was pulled up to stand at the other end of the pool and pray.

While never officially described at Lourdes in baptismal terms, the similarity was powerful. We die to the false self, out of control, and rise with lavish, unpredictable grace bestowing new life. For me, this all was part of an unexpected pilgrimage. Reflecting back, it felt like practice for the real thing, when I step over that final threshold. Baptism is both practice and promise for the journey that dies to self and rises to the embrace of new life, at life's beginning and at its end. The healing waters of Lourdes were also both practice and promise for the end, and new beginning, of my pilgrimage.

For many in the Christian tradition, facing death is supposed to be straightforward. It's simply a matter of faith. God raised Jesus from the dead. And we are raised from death into a new and eternal life. At Lourdes, a Canadian priest gave a homily one morning at Mass, reflecting on what the gospel—or the "Good News"—proclaimed by the apostles really meant. He shared that a serious operation had caused him to spend time in that reflection,

The core message of "Good News," he said, was simply that death had been overcome by Jesus Christ and his resurrection. That's what the creeds say, and what Christians have been taught to believe, by faith. Perhaps that's enough, and for many it is.

In quiet, secluded moments, however, untold numbers who recite those creeds wonder what, if anything, really happens after death. I know I have, and I went through a period of life when the thought of my death struck private terror in my heart. That began to change when I stepped away from my desk in the US Senate offices in 1972 and made that first pilgrimage to the Trappist monastery in Berryville, Virginia. There, in encounters mentioned earlier, I had experiences of feeling surrounded and overcome by the presence of God's love. It was embodied in light. I felt addressed, carried, nearly absorbed. This was palpable and unforgettable to this day, forty-eight years later.

From that time, my life began moving in a different direction. The retreat at Berryville made a transforming difference once I arrived home. Along the way, of course, there have been countless fits and starts, often losing my center, and then withdrawing to recenter my inner life, and my outward journey. But because of that light, I began losing my fear of death—because of that light and the presence of the love that it reflected.

Near-death experiences are frequently characterized by the presence of radiant light. Curiosity about such near-death encounters has grown, with some noted books documenting compelling stories. Most interesting to me are ones written by those considering themselves areligious, such as Dr. Eben Alexander in his *Proof of Heaven*. An excellent neurosurgeon describing himself as skeptical about religion, Dr. Alexander went into a coma when meningitis attacked his brain, a condition almost always fatal. But he reported a vivid encounter with spiritual reality, more real, he writes, than anything he had ever known. In this near presence of God he heard the words, "You are loved and cherished. You have nothing to fear."

His book describes in detail a journey taking him into this realm but then coming back as he recovered and lived to tell and write about it. With nothing to prove, his proof of heaven carries a persuasive credibility. Some like Eben Alexander become unintentional pilgrims who seem to cross over and then return home. They shed and share light for others embarking on this final journey.

At a conference in Santa Fe, I had a conversation with Stephanie Arnold. A young woman not particularly devoted to religious faith, she was facing the birth of her second child. But she received a strong, overwhelming premonition that she would die in childbirth. Doctors could find no cause for alarm and dismissed her concerns, except for one who ordered extra blood to be on hand. During delivery, however, she had an amniotic fluid embolism, pushing her into cardiac arrest. The monitors flatlined for thirty-seven seconds as she died. But with the extra blood, the medical team revived her. Unconscious for six days, she then recovered.

Stephanie began to recall and share the entire experience of her death, which she reported witnessing, accompanied by other beings in the spiritual realm. She was opened to another reality on the other side of death, and then wrote the book *Thirty-Seven Seconds*, trying to recount and explain her encounters. When we met, she was interested in my perspectives as a pastor, even as I was wanting to listen deeply to her experience, where the veil seemed to be pierced for an unsuspecting person in inexplicable ways.

I wonder how Stephanie's experience, and that of Eben Alexander, relate those of Bernadette Soubirous, Bernardo Abyeta, Juan Diego—who had the vision of Our Lady of Guadalupe—or Teresa of Avila, or Julian of Norwich. Were not all of these seeing, through tinted glasses, the same spiritual reality, a hole in the veil?

As with those seventy officially recognized miracles at Lourdes, scientific, rational explanations are illusive. But for the pilgrim embarking on their final journey, these offer some embodied signs that when we relinquish all control and even embrace death, we step into a realm of light saturated with the presence of love.

Mystics have long borne witness to visions of light, punctuating the dark nights of their souls. Many report being held, resting in the presence of an embracing love discovered at the center of our being as God's beloved child, and revealed to be at the center of all things. It can be said that a person is afraid of death for as long as they do not truly know who they are. When our identity is planted in this love, we understand that nothing can ultimately harm us.

At this point in my pilgrim journey, I am often participating in liturgies reciting what we believe, by faith, to be true. But when it comes to assertions about death not being the last word and having faith to believe in the promises of life to come, something within me quietly demurs. It's not a matter of blind faith for me any longer, clinging to words I long to be true. Instead, deep within, mysteriously, I know.

This pilgrimage of life has a final destination. We all reach it, prepared or not. The final step moves off of the ground, whether holy or not, and crosses a river.

When Moses led the oppressed Jewish people out of Egypt and through the Red Sea, they were promised a new land, and they walked as a people to reach that land. Instead, their pilgrimage took them walking in circles in the wilderness for forty years. No yellow arrows pointed the way. They floundered, complained, toyed with deserting Yahweh in the desert, received commandments from their leader's mountaintop experience that they didn't appreciate. But gradually they learned what it meant to be a people trusting in their God and trying to live accordingly. The forty years following their liberation from slavery in some ways may be a metaphor for the four decades following the confinement of our adolescence as we live into adulthood.

It wasn't the Judean wilderness where the people of Israel wandered aimlessly, with holy purpose. Scholars imagine they were in the Sinai desert. Eventually the children of Israel headed further up north into the Promised Land, reaching the Jordan River. But it was at flood stage. The Hebrew Bible records, in the third chapter of Joshua, that the Ark of the Covenant was carried into the river. As if dammed upstream, the river stopped flowing, and the people of Israel then crossed over the Jordan.

Crossing the Jordan has become a metaphor for walking as a pilgrim through the cold waters of death into new life. In the Orthodox Church, at baptism, the priest prays for the blessing specifically of the waters of the Jordan. Just as the people of Israel made this crossing, the baptismal candidate goes through this holy water to surrender to a kind of dying, and to embrace the promise of life made new.

But it's the experience of African Americans that resonated so deeply with the metaphor of crossing the Jordan and shared this in the spiritual songs they sang. This wasn't just "music"; it was real, embodied experience, born out of suffering, and bathed in hope. The late James Cone wrote that going over the Jordan meant that death was a deliverance from slavery and oppression into a heavenly life. But for many it also meant crossing the boundary into the northern "free" states, or Canada:

I'll meet you in the morning
When you reach the promised land
On the other side of the Jordan
For I'm bound for the promised land.

In one song originating from slaves on St. Helens Island in South Carolina, we hear that "Michael rowed the boat ashore." It is the archangel Michael, taking charge of our oars, and getting us across the Jordan:

Jordan's River is chilly and cold, hallelujah
Chills the body but not the soul, hallelujah.

In diverse Christian traditions the hymns and songs sounded out how these waters symbolized the final passage in life's pilgrimage. And it could be a perilous passage, as these words in Isaiah recognize: "When you pass through the waters, I will be with you; and through the rivers, they shall not overwhelm you." We'll have help. In 2006, *The World Beloved: A Bluegrass Mass* was composed by Carol Barnett. Four years later, an album of the same name was released. In this magnificent recording, set in the framework of a Mass, Barnett also uses the image of crossing the River Jordan as the final passage in life's pilgrimage. It's a Credo, appropriately:

Oh, I do believe a place awaits us far across the Jordan
And when we reach those mossy banks, we'll cast aside
    our oars.
Row on, row on, we're crossing River Jordan.
Row on, row on,
And no one goes alone.

We walk, step by step, on paths that become sacred. We dance on ground that is holy. We fill our hands with healing dirt. We sink our bodies and souls into cleansing waters. We are beckoned forward as pilgrims, and in the end, we are carried without oars, over the Jordan, to our final resting place, which is promised land, and a new beginning.

NOTES

CHAPTER 1: THE RESTLESS SOUL

"God walks 'slowly' because he is love."
Kosuke Koyama, *Three Mile an Hour God* (London: SCM Press Ltd., 1979), 7.

CHAPTER 2: REAL PRESENCE

This "irresistible attraction to screens . . ."
Cal Newport, *Digital Minimalism: Choosing a Focused Life in a Noisy World* (New York: Portfolio/Penguin, 2019), xi.

CHAPTER 3: PERSISTENT PATIENCE

"The walking is hard but also simple . . ."
Teresa Pasquale Mateus, "Meditation for Day 19," in *Are We There Yet? Pilgrimage in the Season of Lent* (Cincinnati: Forward Movement, 2017), 77.

CHAPTER 4: THE STRENGTH TO LET GO

I doubt that Bob Buford . . .
Carl Jung's name does appear in one sentence of *Halftime* as a passing reference on page 162.

"We need to be strong enough . . ."
James Hollis, *Finding Meaning in the Second Half of Life: How to Finally, Really Grow Up* (New York: Avery/Penguin, 2005), 153.

CHAPTER 5: WALKING INTO FAITH

"The Word-made-flesh here . . ."
Julie Canlis, "Pilgrimage, Geography, and Mischievous Theology," *The Other Journal* (Seattle School of Theology and Psychology), no. 24 (February 24, 2015): https://tinyurl.com/w6ftdvw.

"base fusing of the physical . . ."
Canlis, "Pilgrimage, Geography, and Mischievous Theology."

"All pilgrimages should be stopped . . ."
James Harpur, *The Pilgrim Journey: A History of Pilgrimage in the Western World* (Katonah, New York: Bluebridge, 2016), 125.

CHAPTER 6: RECKLESS SPIRITUALITY

"Pilgrimage may be thought of . . ."
Victor Turner and Edith Turner, *Image and Pilgrimage in Christian Culture* (New York: Columbia University Press, 1978), 33–34.

"pilgrimage was the great liminal experience . . ."
Turner and Turner, *Image and Pilgrimage*, chap. 1, Kindle.

"A pilgrim is one who divests himself . . ."
Turner and Turner, *Image and Pilgrimage*, chap. 1, Kindle.

CHAPTER 7: UNPREDICTABLE GRACE

"For me," writes Sister Simone Campbell . . .
Adapted from Simone Campbell, "Religion and Politics," *Oneing* 5, no. 2 (Politics and Religion) (Albuquerque, NM: Center for Action and Contemplation, 2017), 58, 59, 61, 62.

"The wandering saints set forth . . ."
Christine Valters Paintner, *The Soul's Slow Ripening: 12 Celtic Practices for Seeking the Sacred* (Notre Dame, IN: Sorin Books, 2018), chap.1, Kindle.

Among the books they mentioned was . . .
Tod Bolsinger, *Canoeing the Mountains: Christian Leadership in Uncharted Territory* (Downers Grove, IL: IVP Books, 2019).

CHAPTER 8: A REENCHANTED WORLD

Later he went on the Camino . . .
Ryan Kuja, "A Pilgrim's Blood and Eschatological Hope," Seattle School of Theology and Psychology, May 19, 2015, https://tinyurl.com/rtcvoel.

"The need for physical, embodied . . ."
Richard Rohr, "The Sacrament of Anointing," Daily Meditations (blog), Center for Action and Contemplation, April 9, 2019, https://tinyurl.com/wbr6lxt.

CHAPTER 9: LEAVING THE EMPIRE BEHIND

"a pilgrimage was a rough test of faith . . ."
Timothy Egan, *A Pilgrimage to Eternity: From Canterbury to Rome in Search of a Faith* (New York: Viking, 2019), 30.

"Sacred pilgrimage is a form of faith . . ."
Kristine Greenaway, *Preparing for a Pilgrimage of Justice and Peace: A Guide for Parishes, Missions, and Ministries* (Geneva: WCC Publications, 2015), 4. PDF file. https://tinyurl.com/qlohqzq.

CHAPTER 10: LEAVING LIFE

"I'll meet you in the morning . . ."
Daniel L. Smith Christopher, "River Jordan in Early African American Spirituals," Bible Odyssey, Society of Biblical Literature, accessed December 17, 2019, https://tinyurl.com/rc6l9or.

FOR FURTHER READING

Boers, Arthur P. *The Way Is Made by Walking: A Pilgrimage along the Camino de Santiago*. Downers Grove, IL: InterVarsity Press, 2007.

Bolsinger, Tod E. *Canoeing the Mountains: Christian Leadership in Uncharted Territory*. Downers Grove, IL: IVP Books/InterVarsity Press, 2018.

Brierley, John. *A Pilgrim's Guide to the Camino de Santiago*. Forres, Scotland: Camino Guides/Findhorn Press, 2017.

Codd, Kevin A. *To the Field of Stars: A Pilgrim's Journey to Santiago de Compostela*. Grand Rapids, MI: Eerdmans, 2008.

Crawford, Kerry. *Lourdes Today: A Pilgrimage to Mary's Grotto*. Cincinnati, OH: Servant Books/St. Anthony Messenger Press, 2008.

Egan, Timothy. *A Pilgrimage to Eternity: From Canterbury to Rome in Search of a Faith*. New York: Viking, 2019.

Harpur, James. *Pilgrim Journey: A History of Pilgrimage in the Western World*. New York: Blueridge/United Tribes Media, 2017.

Hollis, James. *Finding Meaning in the Second Half of Life*. New York: Avery/Penguin, 2006.

Hopkins-Greene, Nancy, et al. *Are We There Yet?: Pilgrimages in the Season of Lent*. Cincinnati, OH: Forward Movement, 2017.

Koyama, Kosuke. *Three Mile an Hour God*. London: SCM Press, 1979.

Newport, Cal. *Digital Minimalism: Choosing a Focused Life in a Noisy World*. New York: Portfolio/Penguin, 2019.

Paintner, Christine Valters. *The Soul's Slow Ripening: 12 Celtic Practices for Seeking the Sacred*. Notre Dame, IN: Sorin Books/Ave Maria Press, 2018.

Palmer, Parker J. *On the Brink of Everything: Grace; Gravity; and Getting Old*. San Francisco: Berrett-Koehler, 2018.

Rohr, Richard. *Falling Upward: A Spirituality for the Two Halves of Life*. London: SPCK, 2013.

Rupp, Joyce. *Walk in a Relaxed Manner: Life Lessons from the Camino*. Maryknoll, NY: Orbis Books, 2005.

Turner, Victor W., and Edith L. B. Turner. *Image and Pilgrimage in Christian Culture*. New York: Columbia University Press, 2011.

ACKNOWLEDGMENTS

It takes a community to write a book. Many have been essential to make this work possible. When Mark Van Oss shared with me the memorable impact of his thirty-five-day pilgrimage on the Camino de Santiago, it spoke to my heart, and I knew I would eventually end up on that ancient path. It took the generous invitation of Kyle Small's sabbatical from Western Theological Seminary to get me there, accompanied by David Patrick King and Mark Carlson for our ten-day journey that wove our lives together.

This book, however, is not another accounting of the Camino; wonderful ones are available and have enriched me. Rather, I've wanted to portray pilgrimages as a portal into embodied faith, guiding our life's journey. Walking many miles with Bill Thompson in and around Santa Fe, New Mexico, helped shape what I wanted to say. My agent, Kathy Helmers, was brilliant in showing me how to frame and focus the book's message. Lil Copan, my editor with Broadleaf Books, has been an indefatigable companion to my writing, always determined to make it better.

My ecumenical commitments have brought the privilege of journeying across the world, including to the Tabieorar Festival in Nigeria, with the generous hospitality of Archbishop and Primate Rufus Ostitelu, as well as to Leipzig, Christiansfeld, and elsewhere described in these pages. I'm very thankful for my work with the Global Christian Forum, the World Communion of Reformed Churches, and the Reformed Church in America.

The Norbortine Abbey outside of Albuquerque, New Mexico, extended its gracious hospitality, and a hermitage, as the place for me to finish putting words on these pages.

My faithful companion in my life's pilgrimage for almost five decades is my wife, Kaarin. She's guided my steps in so many ways, insisting that I go to Lourdes, celebrating my time on the Camino, and knowing that this book, more than any other, comes from my heart. I'm so grateful for our journey together.